CLEP

College Level Examination Program

College
Composition and Modular

Jessica Egan, MS

XAMonline

To obtain permission(s) to use the material from this work for any purpose
including workshops or seminars, please submit a written request to:

XAMonline, Inc.
21 Orient Avenue
Melrose, MA 02176
Toll Free: 1-800-301-4647
Email: info@xamonline.com
Web: www.xamonline.com
Fax: 1-617-583-5552

Library of Congress Cataloging-in-Publication Data
Egan, Jessica

CLEP College Composition/Modular / Jessica Egan
ISBN: 978-1-60787-527-7
1. CLEP   2. Study Guides   3. College Composition/Modular

Disclaimer:
The opinions expressed in this publication are the sole works of XAMonline
and were created independently from the College Board, or other testing
affiliates. Between the time of publication and printing, specific test standards
as well as testing formats and website information may change that are not
included in part or in whole within this product. XAMonline develops sample
test questions, and they reflect similar content as on real tests; however,
they are not former tests. XAMonline assembles content that aligns with test
standards but makes no claims nor guarantees candidates a passing score.

Cover photo provided by iStock.com/stukkey/9957164

Printed in the United States of America
CLEP College Composition and Modular
ISBN: 978-1-60787-527-7

Table of Contents

Meet the Author

Jessica Egan

With a Master's Degree in English Education from Florida State University, Jessica Egan has expertise in the areas of literature, linguistics, and educational psychology. Jessica has worked as an instructional technologist and has experience in teaching secondary English, English as a Second Language (ESL), college-level composition and Adult Basic Education (ABE). She has authored lesson plans, teacher certification materials, and test preparation texts.

About XAMonline

XAMonline – A specialty CLEP publisher

XAMonline – A publisher specializing in CLEP

The College Board CLEP series offers thirty three tests. If your goal is to survey the field and see which of the tests fit into your college curriculum schedule then a good first step resource is XAMonline's

- CLEP 33 ISBN 978-1-60787-575-8

CLEP has clusters of subjects: english; languages, sociology, history, math, science, and business. Each one of these clusters has numerous tests. XAMonline specializes by subject with full length sample tests and explanations.

- CLEP Literature Sampler ISBN 978-1-60787-583-3
- CLEP Foreign Language Sampler ISBN 978-1-60787-577-2
- CLEP Sociology Sampler ISBN 978-1-60787-579-6
- CLEP History Sampler ISBN 978-1-60787-578-9
- CLEP Math Sampler ISBN 978-1-60787-581-9
- CLEP Science Sampler ISBN 978-1-60787-580-2
- CLEP Business Sampler ISBN 978-1-60787-582-6

Another way XAMonline specializes is to focus your attention to what historically has been the most popular tests according to Nielson rankings. CLEP 5 is most popular among civilians, CLEP Military favorites are most popular according to military statistics. Each book comes with numerous tests and full explanations.

- CLEP 5 Favorites ISBN 978-1-60787-576-5
- CLEP Military Favorites ISBN 978-1-60787-551-2

Once you know what specific test you feel most comfortable with you can get a complete picture of your understanding with XAMonline products. True to format content and full length sample tests give you the opportunity to practice under test day conditions. Specialized content is available in the following study guides that will align with all the CLEP standards and you can be assured that you are studying in the most focused way possible.

- CLEP Algebra ISBN 978-1-60787-530-7
- CLEP College Mathematics ISBN 978-1-60787-532-1
- CLEP College Composition/Modular ISBN 978-1-60787-527-7
- CLEP Analyzing and Interpreting Literature ISBN 978-1-60787-526-0

- CLEP Spanish ISBN 978-1-60787-528-4
- CLEP Biology ISBN 978-1-60787-531-4
- CLEP Introductory Psychology ISBN 978-1-60787-529-1

Our competitive advantage

As of 2016, the College Board are administrators of the CLEP Spanish test and do not make full guides for this test or any other test. For Spanish, they offer "official" material that has 100 of the 120 questions. It provided answers but failed to include explanations or content. The material is not a former test. It has no audios to go along with the listening sections. You must decide for yourself if you think a sample test is a study guide or is it a study resource? Is it "Official" if it is not a real test? Is it 2016 if it is essentially the same product as it has been in many past years.

Over the last 20 years, XAMonline has helped nearly 600,000 test takers. Our commitment to preparation exceeds simply providing the proper material for study - it extends to helping you gain mastery of the subject matter, ushering today's students toward a successful future.

Overview of the Test

I. The College-Level Examination Program _____

How the Program Works

CLEP exams are administered at over 1,800 institutions nationwide, and 2,900 colleges and universities award college credit to those who perform well on them. This rigorous program allows many self-directed students of a wide range of ages and backgrounds to demonstrate their mastery of introductory college-level material and pursue greater academic success. Students can earn credit for what they already know by getting qualifying scores on any of the 33 examinations.

The CLEP exams cover material that is taught in introductory-level courses at many colleges and universities. Faculty at individual colleges review the exams to ensure that they cover the important material currently taught in their courses.

Although CLEP is sponsored by the College Board, only colleges may grant credit toward a degree. To learn about a particular college's CLEP policy, contact the college directly. When you take a CLEP exam, you can request that a copy of your score report be sent to the college you are attending or planning to attend. After evaluating your score, the college will decide whether or not to award you credit for a certain course or courses, or to exempt you from them.

If the college decides to give you credit, it will record the number of credits on your permanent record, thereby indicating that you have completed work equivalent to a course in that subject. If the college decides to grant exemption without giving you credit for a course, you will be permitted to omit a course that would normally be required of you and to take a course of your choice instead.

The CLEP program has a long-standing policy that an exam may not be taken within the specified wait period. This waiting period provides you with an opportunity to spend additional time preparing for the exam or the option of taking a classroom course. If you violate the CLEP retest policy, the administration will be considered invalid, the score canceled, and any test fees will be forfeited. If you are a military service member, please note that DANTES will not fund retesting on a previously funded CLEP exam. However, you may personally fund a retest after the specified wait period.

The CLEP Examinations

CLEP exams cover material directly related to specific undergraduate courses taught during a student's first two years in college. The courses may be offered for three, four, six or eight semester hours in general areas such as mathematics, history, social sciences, English composition, natural sciences and humanities. Institutions will either grant credit for a specific course based on a satisfactory score on the related exam, or in the general area in which a satisfactory is earned. The credit is equal to the credit awarded to students who successfully complete the courses. See the Table of Contents for a complete list of all exam titles.

What the Examinations Are Like

CLEP exams are administered on computer and are approximately 90 minutes long, with the exception of College Composition, which is approximately 120 minutes long. Most questions are multiple-choice; other types of questions require you to fill in a numeric answer, to shade areas of an object, or to put items in the correct order. Questions using these kinds of skills are called zone, shade, grid, scale, fraction, numeric entry, histogram and order match questions.

CLEP College Composition includes a mandatory essay section, responses to which must be typed into the computer.

Some of the examinations have optional essays. You should check with the individual college or university where you are sending your score to see whether an optional essay is required for those exams. These essays are administered on paper and are scored by faculty at the institution that receives your score.

Where to Take the Examinations and How to Register

CLEP exams are administered throughout the year at over 1,800 test centers in the United States and select international sites. Once you have decided to take a CLEP examination, you can log into My Account at https://clepportal.collegeboard.org/myaccount to create and manage your own personal accounts, pay for CLEP exams and purchase study materials. You can self-register at any time by completing the online registration form.

Through My Account you can also access a list of institutions that administer CLEP and locate a test center in your area. After paying for your exam through My Account, you must still contact the test center to schedule your CLEP exam.

If you are unable to locate a test center near you, call 800-257-9558 for more information.

ACE's College Credit Recommendation Service

The College Credit Recommendation Service (CREDIT) of the American Council on Education (ACE) enables you to put all of your educational achievements on a secure and universally accepted ACE transcript. All of your ACE-evaluated courses and examinations, including CLEP, appear in an easy-to-read format that includes ACE credit recommendations, descriptions and suggested transfer areas. The service is perfect for candidates who have acquired college credit at multiple ACE-evaluated organizations or credit-by-examination programs. You may have your transcript released at any time to the college of your choice. There is a one-time setup fee of $40 (includes the cost of your first transcript) and a fee of $15 for each transcript requested after release of the first. ACE has an additional transcript service for organizations offering continuing education units.

The College Credit Recommendation Service is offered through ACE's Center for Lifelong Learning. For more than 50 years, ACE has been at the forefront of the evaluation of education and training attained outside the classroom. For more information about ACE CREDIT, contact:

ACE CREDIT
One Dupont Circle, NW
Suite 250
Washington, DC 20036

ACE's Call Center is open Monday to Friday, 8:45 a.m. to 4:45 p.m., and can be reached at 866-205-6267 or CREDIT@ace.nche.edu. Staff are able to assist you with courses and certifications that carry ACE recommendations for both civilian organizations and training obtained through the military.

If you are already registered for an ACE transcript, you can access your records and order transcripts using the ACE Online Transcript System: https://www.acenet.edu/transcripts/.

ACE's Center for Lifelong Learning can be found on the Internet at: http://www.acenet.edu/higher-education.

How Your Score Is Reported

You have the option of seeing your CLEP score immediately after you complete the exam, except in the case of College Composition, for which scores are available four to six weeks after the exam date. Once you choose to see your score, it will be sent automatically to the institution you have designated as a score recipient; it cannot be canceled. You will receive a candidate copy of your score before you leave the test center. If you have tested at the institution that you have designated as a score recipient, it will have immediate access to your test results.

If you do not want your score reported, you may select that as an option at the end of the examination *before the exam is scored.* Once you have selected the option to not view your score, the score is canceled.

The score will not be reported to the institution you have designated, and you will not receive a candidate copy of your score report. You will have to wait the specified wait period before you can take the exam again.

CLEP scores are kept on file for 20 years. During this period, for a small fee, you may have your transcript sent to another college or to anyone else you specify. Your score(s) will never be sent to anyone without your approval.

II. Approaching a College about CLEP _____

The following sections provide a step-by-step guide to learning about the CLEP policy at a particular college or university. The person or office that can best assist you may have a different title at each institution, but the following guidelines will lead you to information about CLEP at any institution.

Adults and other nontraditional students returning to college often benefit from special assistance when they approach a college. Opportunities for adults to return to formal learning in the classroom are now widespread, and colleges and universities have worked hard to make this a smooth process for older students. Many colleges have established special offices that are staffed with trained professionals who understand the kinds of problems facing adults returning to college. If you think you might benefit from such assistance, be sure to find out whether these services are available at your college.

How to Apply for College Credit

Step 1. *Obtain, or access online, the general information catalog and a copy of the CLEP policy from each college you are considering.*

Information about admission and CLEP policies can be obtained on the college's website at clep.collegeboard.org/search/colleges, or by contacting or visiting the admissions office. Ask for a copy of the publication in which the college's complete CLEP policy is explained. Also, get the name and the telephone number of the person to contact in case you have further questions about CLEP.

Step 2. *If you have not already been admitted to a college that you are considering, look at its admission requirements for undergraduate students to see whether you qualify.*

Whether you're applying for college admission as a high school student, transfer student or as an adult resuming a college career or going to college for the first time, you should be familiar with the requirements for admission at the schools you are considering. If you are a nontraditional student, be sure to check whether the school has separate admissions requirements that might apply to you. Some schools are very selective, while others are "open admission."

It might be helpful for you to contact the admissions office for an interview with a counselor. State why you want the interview and ask what documents you should bring with you or send in advance. (These materials may include a high school transcript, transcript of previous college work or completed application for admission.) Make an extra effort to have all the information requested in time for the interview.

During the interview, relax and be yourself. Be prepared to state honestly why you think you are ready and able to do college work. If you have already taken CLEP exams and scored high enough to earn credit, you have shown that you are able to do college work. Mention this achievement to the admissions counselor because it may increase your chances of being accepted. If you have not taken a CLEP exam, you can still improve your chances of being accepted by describing how your job training or independent study has helped prepare you for college-level work. Discuss with the counselor what you have learned from your work and personal experiences.

Step 3. *Evaluate the college's CLEP policy.*

Typically, a college lists all its academic policies, including CLEP policies, in its general catalog or on its website. You will probably find the CLEP policy statement under a heading such as Credit-by-Examination, Advanced Standing, Advanced Placement or External Degree Program. These sections can usually be found in the front of the catalog. You can also check out the institution's CLEP Policy by visiting clep.collegeboard. org/search/colleges.

Many colleges publish their credit-by-examination policies in separate brochures, which are distributed through the campus testing office, counseling center, admissions office or registrar's office. If you find a very general policy statement in the college catalog, seek clarification from one of these offices.

Review the material in the section of this chapter entitled "Questions to Ask about a College's CLEP Policy." Use these guidelines to evaluate the college's CLEP policy. If you have not yet taken a CLEP exam, this evaluation will help you decide which exams to take. Because individual colleges have different CLEP policies, a review of several policies may help you decide which college to attend.

Step 4. *If you have not yet applied for admission, do so as early as possible.*

Most colleges expect you to apply for admission several months before you enroll, and it is essential that you meet the published application deadlines. It takes time to process your application for admission. If you have yet to take a CLEP exam, you may want to take one or more CLEP exams while you are waiting for your application to be processed. Be sure to check the college's CLEP policy beforehand so that you are taking exams your college will accept for credit. You should also find out from the college when to submit your CLEP score(s).

Complete all forms and include all documents requested with your application(s) for admission.

Normally, an admission decision cannot be reached until all documents have been submitted and evaluated. Unless told to do so, do not send your CLEP score(s) until you have been officially admitted.

Step 5. *Arrange to take CLEP exam(s) or to submit your CLEP score(s).*

CLEP exams can be taken at any of the 1,800 test centers world-wide. To locate a test center near you. clep.collegeboard.org/search/test-centers. If you have already taken a CLEP exam, but did not have your score sent to your college, you can have an official transcript sent at any time for a small fee. Fill out the Transcript Request Form included on the same page as your exam score. If you do not have the form, visit clep. collegeboard.org/about/score to download a copy, or call 800-257-9558 to order a transcript using a major credit card. Completed forms should be faxed to 610-628-3726 or sent to the following address, along with a check or money order made payable to CLEP for $20 (this fee is subject to change).

> CLEP Transcript Service
> P.O. Box 6600
> Princeton, NJ 08541-6600

Transcripts will only include CLEP scores for the past 20 years; scores more than 20 years old are not kept on file.

Your CLEP scores will be evaluated, probably by someone in the admissions office, and sent to the registrar's office to be posted on your permanent record once you are enrolled. Procedures vary from college to college, but the process usually begins in the admissions office.

Step 6. *Ask to receive a written notice of the credit you receive for your CLEP score(s).*

A written notice may save you problems later, when you submit your degree plan or file for graduation. In the event that there is a question about whether or not you earned CLEP credit, you will have an official record of what credit was awarded. You may also need this verification of course credit if you meet with an academic adviser before the credit is posted on your permanent record.

Step 7. *Before you register for courses, seek academic advising.*

A discussion with your academic adviser can help you to avoid taking unnecessary courses and can tell you specifically what your CLEP credit will mean to you. This step may be accomplished at the time you enroll. Most colleges have orientation sessions for new students prior to each enrollment period. During orientation, students are usually assigned academic advisers who then give them individual help in developing long-range plans and course schedules for the next semester. In conjunction with this counseling, you may be asked to take some additional tests so that you can be placed at the proper course level.

Questions to Ask about a College's CLEP Policy

Before taking CLEP exams for the purpose of earning college credit, try to find the answers to these questions:

1. *Which CLEP exams are accepted by the college?*
   A college may accept some CLEP exams for credit and not others — possibly not the exams you are considering. For this reason, it is important that you know the specific CLEP exams for which you can receive credit.

2. *Does the college require the optional free-response (essay) section for exams in composition and literature as well as the multiple-choice portion of the CLEP exam you are considering? Will you be required to pass a departmental test such as an essay, laboratory or oral exam in addition to the CLEP multiple-choice exam?*
   Knowing the answers to these questions ahead of time will permit you to schedule the optional free-response or departmental exam when you register to take your CLEP exam.

3. *Is CLEP credit granted for specific courses at the college? If so, which ones?*
   You are likely to find that credit is granted for specific courses and that the course titles are designated in the college's CLEP policy. It is not necessary, however, that credit be granted for a specific course for you to benefit from your CLEP credit. For instance, at many liberal arts colleges, all students must take certain types of courses; these courses may be labeled the core curriculum, general education requirements, distribution requirements or liberal arts requirements. The requirements are often expressed in terms of credit hours. For example, all students may be required to take at least six hours of humanities, six hours of English, three hours of mathematics, six hours of natural science and six hours of social science, with no particular courses in these disciplines specified. In these instances, CLEP credit may be given as "6 hrs. English Credit" or "3 hrs. Math Credit" without specifying for which English or mathematics courses credit has been awarded. To avoid possible disappointment, you should know before taking a CLEP exam what type of credit you can receive or whether you will be exempted from a required course but receive no credit.

4. *How much credit is granted for each exam you are considering, and does the college place a limit On the total amount of CLEP credit you can earn toward your degree?*
Not all colleges that grant CLEP credit award the same amount for individual exams. Furthermore, some colleges place a limit on the total amount of credit you can earn through CLEP or other exams. Other colleges may grant you exemption but no credit toward your degree. Knowing several colleges' policies concerning these issues may help you decide which college to attend. If you think you are capable of passing a number of CLEP exams, you may want to attend a college that will allow you to earn credit for all or most of them. Check out if your institution grants CLEP policy by visiting clep.collegeboard.org/search/colleges.

5. *What is the required score for earning CLEP credit for each exam you are considering?*
Most colleges publish the required scores for earning CLEP credit in their general catalogs or in brochures. The required score may vary from exam to exam, so find out the required score for each exam you are considering.

6. *What is the college's policy regarding prior course work in the subject in which you are considering taking a CLEP exam?*
Some colleges will not grant credit for a CLEP exam if the candidate has already attempted a college-level course closely aligned with that exam. For example, if you successfully completed English 101 or a comparable course on another campus, you will probably not be permitted to also receive CLEP credit in that subject. Some colleges will not permit you to earn CLEP credit for a course that you failed.

7. *Does the college make additional stipulations before credit will be granted?*
It is common practice for colleges to award CLEP credit only to their enrolled students. There are other stipulations, however, that vary from college to college. For example, does the college require you to formally apply for or to accept CLEP credit by completing and signing a form? Or does the college require you to "validate" your CLEP score by successfully completing a more advanced course in the subject? Getting answers to these and other questions will help to smooth the process of earning college credit through CLEP.

III. Preparing to Take CLEP Examinations _____

Test Preparation Tips

1. Familiarize yourself as much as possible with the test and the test situation before the day of the exam. It will be helpful for you to know ahead of time:

   a. how much time will be allowed for the test and whether there are timed subsections. (This information is included in the examination guides and in the CLEP Tutorial video.)

   b. what types of questions and directions appear on the exam. (See the examination guides.)

   c. how your test score will be computed.

   d. in which building and room the exam will be administered.

   e. the time of the test administration.

   f. direction, transit and parking information to the test center.

2. Register and pay your exam fee through My Account at https:// clepportal.collegeboard.org/myaccount and print your registration ticket. Contact your preferred test center to schedule your appointment to test. Your test center may require an additional administration fee. Check with your test center and confirm the amount required and acceptable method of payment.

3. On the day of the exam, remember to do the following.

   a. Arrive early enough so that you can find a parking place, locate the test center, and get settled comfortably before testing begins.

   b. Bring the following with you:

   - completed registration ticket
   - any registration forms or printouts required by the test center. Make sure you have filled out all necessary paperwork in advance of your testing date.
   - a form of valid and acceptable identification. Acceptable identification must:
     - Be government-issued
     - Be an original document — photocopied documents are not acceptable

- Be valid and current — expired documents (bearing expiration dates that have passed) are not acceptable, no matter how recently they may have expired
- Bear the test-taker's full name, in English language characters, exactly as it appears on the
- Registration Ticket, including the order of the names.
- Middle initials are optional and only need to match the first letter of the middle name when present on both the ticket and the identification.
- Bear a recent recognizable photograph that clearly matches the test-taker
- Include the test-taker's signature
- Be in good condition, with clearly legible text and a clearly visible photograph

  Refer to the Exam Day Info page on the CLEP website (http://clep.collegeboard.org/exam-day-info) for more details on acceptable and unacceptable forms of identification.

- military test-takers, bring your Geneva Convention Identification Card. Refer to clep.collegeboard.org/military for additional information on IDs for active duty members, spouses, and civil service civilian employees.
- two number 2 pencils with good erasers. Mechanical pencils are prohibited in the testing room.

  c. Leave all books, papers and notes outside the test center. You will not be permitted to use your own scratch paper; it will be provided by the test center.

  d. Do not take a calculator to the exam. If a calculator is required, it will be built into the testing software and available to you on the computer. The CLEP Tutorial video will have a demonstration on how to use online calculators.

  e. Do not bring a cell phone or other electronic devices into the testing room.

4. When you enter the test room:

  a. You will be assigned to a computer testing station. If you have special needs, be sure to communicate them to the test center administrator *before* the day you test.

b. Be relaxed while you are taking the exam. Read directions carefully and listen to all instructions given by the test administrator. If you don't understand the directions, ask for help before the test begins. If you must ask a question that is not related to the exam after testing has begun, raise your hand and a proctor will assist you. The proctor cannot answer questions related to the exam.

c. Know your rights as a test-taker. You can expect to be given the full working time allowed for taking the exam and a reasonably quiet and comfortable place in which to work. If a poor testing situation is preventing you from doing your best, ask whether the situation can be remedied. If it can't, ask the test administrator to report the problem on a Center Problem Report that will be submitted with your test results. You may also wish to immediately write a letter to CLEP, P.O. Box 6656, Princeton, NJ 08541- 6656. Describe the exact circumstances as completely as you can. Be sure to include the name of the test center, the test date and the name(s) of the exam(s) you took.

Accommodations for Students with Disabilities

If you have a disability, such as a learning or physical disability, that would prevent you from taking a CLEP exam under standard conditions, you may request accommodations at your preferred test center. Contact your preferred test center well in advance of the test date to make the necessary arrangements and to find out its deadline for submission of documentation and approval of accommodations. Each test center sets its own guidelines in terms of deadlines for submission of documentation and approval of accommodations.

Accommodations that can be arranged directly with test centers include:

- ZoomText (screen magnification)
- Modifiable screen colors
- Use of a reader, amanuensis, or sign language interpreter
- Extended time
- Untimed rest breaks

If the above accommodations do not meet your needs, contact CLEP Services at clep@info.collegeboard.org for information about other accommodations.

IV. Interpreting Your Scores _____

CLEP score requirements for awarding credit vary from institution to institution. The College Board, however, recommends that colleges refer to the standards set by the American Council on Education (ACE). All ACE recommendations are the result of careful and periodic review by evaluation teams made up of faculty who are subject-matter experts and technical experts in testing and measurement. To determine whether you are eligible for credit for your CLEP scores, you should refer to the policy of the college you will be attending. The policy will state the score that is required to earn credit at that institution. Many colleges award credit at the score levels recommended by ACE. However, some require scores that are higher or lower than these.

Your exam score will be printed for you at the test center immediately upon completion of the examination, unless you took College Composition. For this exam, you will receive your score four to six weeks after the exam date. Your CLEP exam scores are reported only to you, unless you ask to have them sent elsewhere. If you want your scores sent to a college, employer or certifying agency, you must select this option through My Account. This service is free only if you select your score recipient at the time you register to take your exam. A fee will be charged for each score recipient you select at a later date. Your scores are kept on file for 20 years. For a fee, you can request a transcript at a later date.

The pamphlet *What Your CLEP Score Means*, which you will receive with your exam score, gives detailed information about interpreting your scores. A copy of the pamphlet is in the appendix of this Guide. A brief explanation appears below.

How CLEP Scores Are Computed

In order to reach a total score on your exam, two calculations are performed.

First, your "raw score" is calculated. This is the number of questions you answer correctly. Your raw score is increased by one point for each question you answer correctly, and no points are gained or lost when you do not answer a question or answer it incorrectly.

Second, your raw score is converted into a "scaled score" by a statistical process called *equating*. Equating maintains the consistency of standards for test scores over time by adjusting for slight differences in difficulty between test forms. This ensures that your score does not depend on the specific test form you took or how well others did on the same form. Your raw score is converted to a scaled score that ranges from 20, the lowest, to 80, the highest. The final scaled score is the score that appears on your score report.

How Essays Are Scored

The College Board arranges for college English professors to score the essays written for the College Composition exam. These carefully selected college faculty members teach at two- and four-year institutions nationwide. The faculty members receive extensive training and thoroughly review the College Board scoring policies and procedures before grading the essays. Each essay is read and scored by two professors, the sum of the two scores for each essay is combined with the multiple-choice score, and the result is reported as a scaled score between 20 and 80. Although the format of the two sections is very different, both measure skills required for expository writing. Knowledge of formal grammar, sentence structure and organizational skills are necessary for the multiple-choice section, but the emphasis in the free-response section is on writing skills rather than grammar.

Optional essays for CLEP Composition Modular and the literature examinations are evaluated and scored by the colleges that require them, rather than by the College Board. If you take an optional essay, it will be sent to the institution you designate when you take the test. If you did not designate a score recipient institution when you took an optional essay, you may still select one as long as you notify CLEP within 18 months of taking the exam. Copies of essays are not held beyond 18 months or after they have been sent to an institution

Description of the Examination

The CLEP College Composition examinations assess writing skills taught in most first-year college composition courses. Those skills include analysis, argumentation, synthesis, usage, ability to recognize logical development and research. The exams cannot cover every skill (such as keeping a journal or peer editing) required in many first-year college writing courses. Candidates will, however, be expected to apply the principles and conventions used in longer writing projects to two timed writing assignments and to apply the rules of standard written English.

College Composition contains multiple-choice items and two mandatory, centrally scored essays. College English faculty from throughout the country convene twice a month to score the essays via an online scoring system. Each of the two essays is scored independently by two different readers, and the scores are then combined. This combined score is weighted approximately equally with the score from the multiple-choice section. These scores are then combined to yield the candidate's score. The resulting combined score is reported as a single scaled score between 20 and 80. Separate scores are not reported for the multiple-choice and essay sections. College Composition contains approximately 50 multiple-choice items to be answered in 50 minutes and two essays to be written in 70 minutes, for a total of 120 minutes testing time.

Knowledge and Skills Required

The exam measures candidates' knowledge of the fundamental principles of rhetoric and composition and their ability to apply the principles of standard written English. In addition, the exam requires familiarity with research and reference skills. In one of the essays, candidates must develop a position by building an argument in which they synthesize information from two provided sources, which they must cite. The requirement that candidates cite the sources they use reflects the recognition of source attribution as an essential skill in college writing courses.

College Composition

The skills assessed in the College Composition examination follow. The numbers preceding the main topics indicate the approximate percentages of exam questions on those topics. The bulleted lists under each topic are meant to be representative rather than prescriptive.

10% Conventions of Standard Written English

This section measures candidates' awareness of a variety of logical, structural and grammatical relationships within sentences. The questions test recognition of acceptable usage relating to the items below:

- Syntax (parallelism, coordination, subordination)
- Sentence boundaries (comma splice, run-ons, sentence fragments)
- Recognition of correct sentences

- Concord/agreement (pronoun reference, case shift, and number; subject-verb; verb tense)
- Diction
- Modifiers
- Idiom
- Active/passive voice
- Lack of subject in modifying word group
- Logical comparison
- Logical agreement
- Punctuation

40% Revision Skills

This section measures candidates' revision skills in the context of works in progress (early drafts of essays):
- Organization
- Evaluation of evidence
- Awareness of audience, tone and purpose
- Level of detail
- Coherence between sentences and paragraphs
- Sentence variety and structure
- Main idea, thesis statements and topic sentences
- Rhetorical effects and emphasis
- Use of language
- Evaluation of author's authority and appeal
- Evaluation of reasoning
- Consistency of point of view
- Transitions
- Sentence-level errors primarily relating to the conventions of standard written English

25% Ability to Use Source Materials

This section measures candidates' familiarity with elements of the following basic reference and research skills, which are tested primarily in sets but may also be tested through stand-alone questions. In the passage-based sets, the elements listed under Revision Skills and Rhetorical Analysis may also be tested. In addition, this section will cover the following skills:

- Use of reference materials
- Evaluation of sources
- Integration of resource material
- Documentation of sources (including, but not limited to, MLA, APA and Chicago manuals of style)

25% Rhetorical Analysis

This section measures candidates' ability to analyze writing. This skill is tested primarily in passage-based questions pertaining to critical thinking, style, purpose, audience and situation:

- Appeals
- Tone
- Organization/structure
- Rhetorical effects
- Use of language
- Evaluation of evidence

The Essays

In addition to the multiple-choice section, College Composition includes a mandatory essay section that tests skills of argumentation, analysis and synthesis. This section of the exam consists of two essays, both of which measure a candidate's ability to write clearly and effectively. The first essay is based on the candidate's reading, observation or experience, while the second requires candidates to synthesize and cite two sources that are provided. Candidates have 30 minutes to write the first essay and 40 minutes to read the two sources and write the second essay. The essays must be typed on the computer.

Competency 1: Conventions of Standard Written English

Skill 1.1: Syntax (parallelism, coordination, subordination)_____

Syntax is the deliberate order and arrangement of words in a sentence. It takes into account grammatical rules and structure needed for the sentence to have meaning. Words must be arranged in a specific way in order to convey the correct message.

Parallelism includes the concept of presenting ideas as equal thoughts. When ideas are listed in a parallel manner, the sentence flows and emphasis is shared across each idea. In contrast, when ideas are listed without parallelism, the sentence becomes choppy and incomprehensible.

Example:

> Before boarding the plane she said goodbye to her husband, bought a coffee and went through the security checkpoint. *(parallel)*

> Before boarding the plane she said goodbye to her husband, stopped at the coffee stand that had just opened for a drink, and went through the security checkpoint. *(non-parallel)*

Coordination and subordination combine ideas to give emphasis on a particular portion of a sentence. Coordination includes a coordinating conjunction and subordination includes a subordinating conjunction. Using either of these methods can change the emphasis of ideas and overall meaning of the sentence.

Coordinating conjunctions emphasize equal ideas: and, but, or, etc.

Subordinating conjunctions emphasize main ideas: although, because, before, though, etc.

Example:

> The restaurant had a hostess, and they decided to keep the podium at the front door. *(coordination)*

> The restaurant decided to keep the podium at the front door, because they had a hostess. *(subordination)*

Skill 1.2: Sentence boundaries (comma splice, run-ons, sentence fragments) ⎯⎯⎯⎯⎯⎯

Comma splices appear when two sentences are joined by only a comma. Run-on sentences, also known as fused sentences, appear when two sentences are run together with no punctuation at all. Fragments include a portion of a sentence, but they do not represent a complete thought. Complete sentences must include a subject (noun), predicate (verb), and they must represent a complete thought.

Examples:

a) *Error:* Dr. Sanders is a brilliant scientist, his research on genetic disorders won him a Nobel Prize.

   Problem: A comma alone cannot join two independent clauses (complete sentences). The two clauses can be joined by a semi-colon, or they can be separated by a period.

   Correction: Dr. Sanders is a brilliant scientist; his research on genetic disorders won him a Nobel Prize.

   --- OR ---

   Correction: Dr. Sanders is a brilliant scientist. His research on genetic disorders won him a Nobel Prize.

b) *Error:* Florida is noted for its beaches they are long, sandy, and beautiful.

   Problem: The first sentence ends with the word beaches, and the second sentence cannot be joined with the first. The fused sentence error can be corrected in several ways: (1) one clause may be made dependent on another with a subordinating conjunction or a relative pronoun; (2) a semi-colon may be used to combine two equally important ideas; (3) the two independent clauses may be separated by a period.

   Correction: Florida is noted for its beaches, which are long, sandy, and beautiful.

   --- OR ---

   Correction: Florida is noted for its beaches; they are long, sandy, and beautiful.

   --- OR ---

   Correction: Florida is noted for its beaches. They are long, sandy, and beautiful.

c) *Error:* Worked on the garage.

Problem: This is a fragment because there is no subject and this does not represent and complete thought. You may be asking yourself: who worked on the garage?

Correction: John worked on the garage.

Skill 1.3: Recognition of correct sentences ⎯⎯⎯⎯

A fact is something that is true and can be proved.

An opinion is something that a person believes, thinks, or feels.

Examine the following examples:

Joe DiMaggio, a Yankees' center-fielder, was replaced by Mickey Mantle in 1952.
This is a fact. If necessary, evidence can be produced to support this.

First year players are more ambitious than seasoned players.
This is an opinion. There is no proof to support that everyone feels this way.

Skill 1.4: Concord/agreement (pronoun reference, case shift, and number; subject-verb; verb tense) ⎯

A pronoun must correspond with the singular or plural form of the noun, called the antecedent, to which it refers. Similarly, a pronoun must be in the same person (1st,2nd, 3rd) as the noun. A pronoun must refer clearly to a single word, not to a complete idea.

Pronouns, unlike nouns, change case forms. Pronouns must be in the subjective, objective, or possessive form according to their function in the sentence.

Example:

Error: A teacher should treat all their students fairly.

Problem: Since A teacher is singular, the pronoun referring to it must also be singular. Otherwise, the noun has to be made plural.

Correction: Teachers should treat all their students fairly.

For proper subject-verb agreement, a verb must correspond in the singular or plural form with the simple subject; it is not affected by any interfering elements.

Note: A simple subject is never found in a prepositional phrase (a phrase beginning with a word such as of, by, over, through, until).

Example:

> *Error:* Either the police captain or his officers is going to the convention.
>
> *Problem:* In either/or and neither/nor constructions, the verb agrees with the subject closer to it.
>
> *Correction:* Either the police captain or his officers are going to the convention.

Skill 1.5: Diction

Diction includes the deliberate selection of words to convey meaning. The message can be emphasized in the style of writing or through emphasis when read orally. The enunciation of selected words has the potential to emphasize meaning, and an accent may make the meaning difficult to understand.

For example, a passage read quickly in a New York accent may be difficult to understand, but it may convey that the passage resembles a time or place in New York. This can be critical to the context and character development. The same goes for a Shakespearean play. Words are most likely enunciated to provide emphasis in meaning in the script. This draws in the audience and assists them in comprehending the author's intended message.

Skill 1.6: Modifiers

Particular phrases that are not placed near the one word they modify often result in misplaced modifiers. Particular phrases that do not relate to the subject being modified result in dangling modifiers.

Example:

> *Error:* Weighing the options carefully, a decision was made regarding the punishment of the convicted murderer.
>
> *Problem:* Who is weighing the options? No one capable of weighing is named in the sentence; thus, the participle phrase weighing the options

carefully dangles. This problem can be corrected by adding a subject of the sentence capable of doing the action.

Correction: Weighing the options carefully, the judge made a decision regarding the punishment of the convicted murderer.

Skill 1.7: Idiom

Dependent to figurative language, idioms are phrases that typically do not represent a literal meaning. They are created by native speakers and are not predictable by breaking down elements within the phrase. For example, a "birthday suit" has nothing to do with a birthday or a suit.

Examples:

Beat around the bush	Whole nine yards
Straw that broke the camel's back	Jump the gun
Hit the nail on the head	Sick as a dog
Killed two birds with one stone	On thin ice
Piece of cake	Kick the bucket

Skill 1.8: Active/passive voice

The difference between active and passive voice lies in the action of sentence. When the subject performs the action, the sentence is using active voice. When the subject is acted upon by the verb, it is considered passive voice.

Example:

He opened the window.
Active voice

The window was opened by him as it began to rain.
Passive voice

Note: It is common for sentences using active voice to be brief and concise, while the passive voice is typically a more lengthy sentence.

Skill 1.9: Lack of subject in modifying word group

There are times when a subject may be implied. To find the subject, a reader often ask themselves "who" or "what" is completing the action. For example, if a sentence said, "The girl watches a movie" we are able to question who is completing the action for the very "watching." It's clear to see that the girl is the subject in this sentence.

For a sentence such as "Sit down and watch the movie," we can infer that the subject could be the word "you." Other examples include:

(You) Watch your brother.

(You) Don't forget to bring an umbrella.

The reader can use context clues and point of view to quickly determine an implied subject.

See also Skill 1.6.

Skill 1.10: Logical comparison

In order to draw logical comparisons and make conclusions, a reader must use prior knowledge and apply it to the current situation. A conclusion or inference is never stated. You must rely on your common sense.

Read the following passage.

> The Smith family waited patiently around carousel number 7 for their luggage to arrive. They were exhausted after their 5 hour trip and were anxious to get to their hotel. After about an hour, they realized that they no longer recognized any of the other passengers' faces. Mrs. Smith asked the person who appeared to be in charge if they were at the right carousel. The man replied, "Yes, this is it, but we finished unloading that baggage almost half an hour ago."

From the man's response we can infer that:

(A) The Smiths were ready to go to their hotel.

(B) The Smith's luggage was lost.

(C) The man had their luggage.

(D) They were at the wrong carousel.

Since the Smiths were still waiting for their luggage, we know that they were not yet ready to go to their hotel. From the man's response, we know that they were not at the wrong carousel and that he did not have their luggage. Therefore, though not directly stated, it appears that their luggage was lost. Choice (B) is the correct answer.

Skill 1.11: Logical agreement

Similar to logical comparison (Skill 1.10), logical agreement draws on prior knowledge. In addition for the conclusion to be logical, the grammatical makeup of the sentences must be logical as well.

Logical- can be proven. (Factual)
Non-logical- cannot be proven. (Opinion)
Illogical- Can be proven wrong. (Factual)

To test for logic, a reader can put the scenario in a logical sequence, called the syllogism.

Claim: All leaves turn yellow in autumn.
Claim: Maple trees have leaves.
Agreement: The leaves on maple trees turn yellow in autumn.

Skill 1.12: Punctuation

Commas

Commas indicate a brief pause. They are used to set off dependent clauses and long introductory word groups. They are also used to separate words in a series. They are used to set off unimportant material that interrupts the flow of the sentence, and they separate independent clauses joined by conjunctions.

a) *Error:* After I finish my master's thesis I plan to work in Chicago.

   Problem: A comma is needed after an introductory dependent word-group containing a subject and verb.

   Correction: After I finish my master's thesis, I plan to work in Chicago.

b) *Error:* I washed waxed and vacuumed my car today.

   Problem: Words in a series should be separated by commas. Although the word *and* is sometimes considered optional, it is often necessary to clarify the meaning.

   Correction: I washed, waxed, and vacuumed my car today.

c) *Error:* She was a talented dancer but she is mostly remembered for her singing ability.

   Problem: A comma is needed before a conjunction that joins two independent clauses (complete sentences).

Correction: She was a talented dancer but she is mostly remembered for her singing ability.

Semicolons and Colons

Semicolons are needed to divide two or more closely related independent sentences.

They are also needed to separate items in a series containing commas. Colons are used to introduce lists and to emphasize what follows.

a) *Error:* I climbed to the top of the mountain, it took me three hours.

Problem: A comma alone cannot separate two independent clauses. Instead a semicolon is needed to separate two related sentences.

Correction: I climbed to the top of the mountain; it took me three hours.

b) *Error:* In the movie, asteroids destroyed Dallas, Texas, Kansas City, Missouri, and Boston, Massachusetts.

Problem: Semicolons are needed to separate items in a series that already contains commas.

Correction: In the movie, asteroids destroyed Dallas, Texas; Kansas City, Missouri; and Boston, Massachusetts.

c) *Error:* Essays will receive the following grades, A for excellent, B for good, C for average, and D for unsatisfactory.

Problem: A colon is needed to emphasize the information or a list that follows.

Correction: Essays will receive the following grades: A for excellent, B for good, C for average, and D for unsatisfactory.

Apostrophes

Apostrophes are used to show either contractions or possession.

a) *Error:* She shouldnt be permitted to smoke cigarettes in the building.

Problem: An apostrophe is needed in a contraction in place of the missing letter.

Correction: She shouldn't be permitted to smoke cigarettes in the building.

b) *Error:* The childrens new kindergarten teacher was also a singer.

Problem: An apostrophe is needed to show possession.

Correction: The childrens' new kindergarten teacher was also a singer.

Note: The apostrophe after the s indicates that there are multiple children.

Quotation Marks

Use double quotation marks to enclose a direct quotation and to enclose the title of an article, a song, an essay, or a short story.

a) *Error:* Franklin Roosevelt once said, There is nothing to fear but fear itself.

Problem: Double quotation marks are needed to set off the quotation.

Correction: Franklin Roosevelt once said, "There is nothing to fear but fear itself".

b) *Error:* In his best-selling novel The Firm, published in 1991, author John Grisham probed the sinister doings in a Memphis law firm.

Problem: Double quotation marks are needed to set off the title of an article.

Correction: In his best-selling novel, "The Firm", published in 1991, author John Grisham probed the sinister doings in a Memphis law firm.

Competency 2: Revision Skills

Skill 2.1: Organization

The organizational pattern of a piece of writing is the way in which the author conveys the main idea and details. A list of organizational patterns commonly used on the test is given below.

Addition - development of a subject point by point.

Cause and Effect - demonstration of how an event came about due to certain conditions or causes.

Classification - division of a subject into different categories or classes.

Comparison and Contrast - pointing out of similarities and/or differences.

Definition - explanation or clarification of the meaning of a word or term.

Explanation - explanation of something said earlier.

Generalization - making of a general statement, which includes the support of specific examples.

Order - listing in order of things or events; may be in order of time, importance or some other element.

Simple Listing - listing of items in no particular order.

Summary - summation of what has already been said in greater detail.

Skill 2.2: Evaluation of evidence

Bias is defined as an opinion, feeling or influence that strongly favors one side in an argument. A statement or passage is biased if an author attempts to convince a reader of something. On the test, the terms valid and invalid have special meaning for the evaluation of evidence. If an argument is valid, it is reasonable. It is objective (not biased) and can be supported by evidence. If an argument is invalid, it is not reasonable. It is not objective. In other words, one can find evidence of bias.

Read the following passage:

Most dentists agree that Bright Smile Toothpaste is the best for fighting cavities. It tastes good and leaves your mouth minty fresh.

Is this a valid or invalid argument?

(A) valid

(B) invalid

It is invalid (B). It mentions that "most" dentists agree. What about those who do not agree? The author is clearly exhibiting bias in leaving those who disagree out.

See also Skill 4.6.

Skill 2.3: Awareness of audience, tone and purpose

Audience, tone and purpose have an impact on the overall message that writing conveys. When analyzing a piece of writing, ask yourself who the content would be directed towards to assist you in determining audience. Also ask yourself the reason behind the author's message to determine the purpose. The tone may also assist you in determining the purpose.

The author's tone is his or her attitude as reflected in the statement or passage. His or her choice of words will help the reader determine the overall tone of a statement or passage.

Read the following paragraph:

I was shocked by your article, which said that sitting down to breakfast was a thing of the past. Many families consider breakfast time, family time. Children need to realize the importance of having a good breakfast. It is imperative that they be taught this at a young age. I cannot believe that a writer with your reputation has difficulty comprehending this.

The author's tone in this passage is one of:

(A) concern

(B) anger

(C) excitement

(D) disbelief

Since the author directly states that he "cannot believe" that the writer feels this way, the answer is (D) disbelief.

Skill 2.4: Level of detail

Supporting details are sentences that give more information about the topic and the main idea. The level of detail will be deliberate in assisting readers in comprehending the material. Some authors leave content up for interpretation, while others provide a high level of detail.

Skill 2.5: Coherence between sentences and paragraphs

Relationships within and between sentences are usually of the same types as the author's overall organizational patterns (see section 2.1). You should become familiar with these types as they will help you determine several types of relationships.

Read the following passage:

> The witness appeared to be troubled by the lawyer's questions. As a result, the jury had no choice but to doubt the witness' testimony.

Which of the following best describes the relationship between the first and second sentence?

(A) Summary

(B) Explanation

(C) Definition

(D) Cause and Effect

Because of the witness' questionable testimony, the jury had no choice but to doubt him. This is clearly a cause and effect relationship. Therefore, answer (D) is the best choice.

Skill 2.6: Sentence variety and structure

Paragraphs should contain variety to enhance the writing. Sentence variety can include difference sentence types, patterns, lengths and structure. Redundant sentence types alter the rhythm of a piece of writing and could impact the flow of the paragraphs to the reader.

For example, a paragraph with simply declarative sentences may sound choppy compared to sentences with variety.

Compare the following:

I like mountains. They are pretty. Sunsets are beautiful on mountains. Hiking on mountains is fun. It's one of my favorite activities.

I like mountains. They are very pretty, and I especially enjoy watching beautiful sunsets from a mountaintop. I also believe hiking is a lot of fun and one of my favorite activities.

Skill 2.7: Main idea, thesis statements and topic sentences

While the topic of a paragraph or story is what the paragraph or story is about, the main idea of a paragraph or story states the important idea(s) that the author wants the reader to know about a topic. Typically found at the end of the first paragraph, a thesis statement reveals the main idea.

The topic and main idea of a paragraph or story are sometimes directly stated. There are times; however, that the topic and main idea are not directly stated, but simply implied.

Example:

Henry Ford was an inventor who developed the first affordable automobile. The cars that were being built before Mr. Ford created his Model-T were very expensive. Only rich people could afford to have cars.

The topic of this paragraph is Henry Ford. The main idea is that Henry Ford built the first affordable automobile.

Skill 2.8: Rhetorical effects and emphasis

Rhetoric organizes language in a certain manner to provide deliberate emphasis. When revising, an author can reorganize thoughts with the intention of persuading a reader. Emphasis can be added through repetition, adding adjectives, adding adverbs, capital letters and with punctuation.

Example:

The book was really boring.

The book was really, really, really boring.

The book was REALLY boring.

The book was really boring!

Throughout the revision process, an author can continue to alter word choices and sentence structures in order to achieve the rhetoric desired to convince their readers. They could enhance their perspective with logic as to why their point is correct, try to determine their audience and create an emotional appeal that the audience could relate to, and improve the vision that their reader might have towards them by altering the writing to have a more inviting, trustworthy tone. One might include two or three drafts throughout the revision process, adding more emphasis and appeal with each edition.

See also Skill 4.4.

Skill 2.9: Use of language

Depending on the piece of writing, the revision process should lead the author to consider how their work is being understood. Similar to rhetoric, the use of language has a great deal of impact on how writing is interpreted. You may have heard the phrase "show, don't tell." This implies painting a picture for a reader to interpret instead of outright stating your thoughts. This especially works well for creative and abstract writing.

For nonfiction and research papers, the use of language should be clear and concise. Considering the audience, the tone would be formal and there would be minimal interpretation for the reader.

Skill 2.10: Evaluation of author's authority and appeal

Considering the authority of an author may give you a greater understanding of the accuracy of their writing and the intention behind it. An author may have more than one purpose in writing. An author's purpose may be to entertain, to persuade, to inform, to describe, or to narrate.

There are no tricks or rules to follow in attempting to determine an author's purpose. It is up to the reader to use his or her judgment.

Read the following paragraph:

> Charles Lindbergh had no intention of becoming a pilot. He was enrolled in the University of Wisconsin until a flying lesson changed the entire course of his life. He began his career as a pilot by performing daredevil stunts at fairs.

The author wrote this paragraph primarily to:

(A) Describe

(B) Inform

(C) Entertain

(D) Narrate

Since the author is simply telling us or informing us about the life of Charles Lindbergh, the correct answer here is (B).

Skill 2.11: Evaluation of reasoning

In addition to the consideration of an author's authority and purpose, a reader should also analyze and evaluate the content. Considering the source (academic article vs. website) and its credibility is a first step to breaking down the reliability of reasoning within the writing.

There is also a certain amount of logic involved in evaluating reasoning. Unrealistic or opinionated content may be easy to identify, but a reader must also pay attention to phrases such as "typically" and "for the most part". Phrases such as this imply factual information and lead the reader to believe the content without actually supplying the facts.

See also Skill 2.2

Skill 2.12 :Consistency of point of view

There are three types of point of view: first, second, and third person. When written in first person, a piece of writing may have an opinionated perspective. Words that indicate first person include: me, my, and I. Writing from a first person point of view impacts the tone (Skill 2.3) and may create bias (Skill 2.2).

Examples:

I like red roses.
First person

You like red roses.
Second person

She likes red roses.
Third person

A piece of writing must stay consistent in point of view throughout. It's not possible for a piece to convey thoughts and opinions from more than one perspective.

Skill 2.13: Transitions

Transitions assist readers in moving from one idea to another by connecting thoughts and phrases. Typically found at the beginning of a paragraph, transitions may introduce a thought, indicate a relationship between thoughts, and show a consequence.

Examples:

In addition	Consequently	Initially
Similarly	Although	Overall
In contrast	Therefore	Specifically

Skill 2.14: Sentence-level errors primarily relating to the conventions of standard written English

Incorrect grammar and usage of language can lead to errors in writing. Common sentence-level errors include lack of capitalization, punctuation, and incomplete thoughts. There are many simple mistakes that a word processor will pick up on, however, they are not programmed to assist in identifying all grammatical errors. The revision process can be utilized to eliminate all errors to ensure the writing follows grammatical rules and conventions of standard written English. In addition to reading the writing for accuracy, reading the piece aloud may assist in zeroing in on errors.

Competency 3: Ability to Use Source Materials

Skill 3.1: Use of reference materials _____

College papers typically require a minimum of 2-3 reference materials for support. There are times when reference materials may be required from a number of categories as well. For example, a 3-5 page paper may require one textbook, two academic articles, and two websites to support your thesis statement. For information about evaluating and integrating reference materials, continue on to Skills 3.2 and 3.3.

Skill 3.2: Evaluation of sources _____

Date: Outdated sources are often viewed as not credible. When selecting a source, it's best to incorporate material that has been written within the past three years.

Credibility of author: Because sources can vary in their originality, try to locate the original source. An author's thoughts about a work may incorporate bias and take away from the intended meaning. Using the original source will assist in making the strongest claim possible.

Source type: Not all information is created equal when it comes to writing papers. Some assignments require the use of specific types of sources, which assists in zeroing in on quality information. Assignments might also specify which sources will be considered unacceptable, such as Wikipedia. When going through the process of selecting sources, consider the following list:

Acceptable sources:

- Scholarly books
- Academic articles (ideally peer reviewed)
- Published thesis
- Historical documents
- College websites
- Newspapers

Poor sources:

- Wikipedia
- Ask.com
- Wordpress

Skill 3.3: Integration of resource material _____

It's important to not overload writing with cited material, and instead, use citations to support your claim. For example, you wouldn't want to include a quote or passage that was 1.5 pages long in a 3 page paper. Instead, you could cut the quote down or include just a portion of the passage in order to support your claim. You can use punctuation, such as an ellipses (...) to shorten the content to an appropriate length.

An example might be comparing historical documents to show the difference of the "Pledge of Allegiance" over the past 100 years. Instead of including the entire passage each time, one might use an ellipses to zero in on the portion that demonstrates the changes.

> "I pledge allegiance to my Flag and the Republic for which it stands, one nation, indivisible, with liberty and justice for all." (1892)

> "I pledge allegiance to the Flag and *to* the Republic for which it stands..." (1923)

> "I pledge allegiance to *the* Flag of the *United States of America...*" (1954)

> "I pledge allegiance to *the* Flag of the United States of America, and to the Republic for which it stands, *one Nation under God...*" (1956)

Another example could include an excerpt from Dr. Martin Luther King's speech being integrated into a paper on racism in America. Including the entire speech would take away from the meaning of the paper, but including a small portion to support a claim could provide excellent support.

> Many of Dr. King's claims can still be understood in modern times. Because there problem of race discrimination has not fully diminished, one might agree that "One hundred years later, the life of the Negro is still sadly crippled by the manacles of segregation and the chains of discrimination." (King, 1963)

Skill 3.4: Documentation of sources (including, but not limited to, MLA, APA and Chicago manuals of style)_____

There are multiple ways to document the sources that you've used in your writing. You not only have to cite the source within the document, you also have to provide a list of references at the end of your paper. This is often referred to as a bibliography or works cited.

Styles vary greatly depending on the type of writing. The Modern Language Association (MLA) is geared towards liberal arts and humanities, while the American Psychological Association (APA) includes social sciences. Citing the same source will require different information and formatting for each.

APA

> In-text citations require the year of publication. For example, "Burke expressed that his involvement in the crime had not gone further than withholding evidence (2011)."
>
> *Reference lists follow these guidelines:*
> Author, A. (Year of publication). Title: Capital letter for first word in subtitle. Location: Publisher.
>
> Example:
> Milner, J., Milner, L. (2011). Bridging English. New York, NY. Pearson Education.

MLA

> In-text citations require the page number. If using the same quote mentioned in the APA example above, you would simply swap out the publication year for the page number: "Burke expressed that his involvement in the crime had not gone further than withholding evidence (373)."
>
> *Reference lists follow these guidelines:*
> Last name, First name. Title of Book. City of Publication: Publisher, Year of Publication. Medium of Publication.
>
> Example:
> Milner, Joseph., Milner, Lucy. Bridging English. New York: Pearson Education, 2011. Print.

Competency 4:
Rhetorical Analysis

Skill 4.1: Appeals

Ethos: credibility of the source. This includes the author's authority and ethical approach to their writing.

Pathos: emotional appeal. This includes specific details, and intense, emotional and empathetic language.

Logos: logic used to support author's claim. This is also inclusive of research that has been included to support their perspective.

See also Skill 2.8.

Skill 4.2: Tone

See Skill 2.3.

Skill 4.3: Organization/structure

See Skill 2.1.

Skill 4.4: Rhetorical effects

In analyzing rhetoric, one would break down a piece of writing to zero in on intentional alterations that the author made to enhance the writing. The author's point of view must be taken into account, in addition to their perspective on the information that's being presented.

Rhetoric is most commonly used in persuasive writing. This writing can be exaggerated and riddled with opinions, so it is important for the reader to think critically and question the content and credibility of the author's deliberate use of rhetoric while reading.

See also Skill 2.8.

Skill 4.5: Use of language

See Skill 2.9.

Skill 4.6: Evaluation of evidence

In addition to determining the authority of the author (Skill 2.10) and whether or not there is bias (Skill 2.2) in their writing, readers must also evaluate evidence that has been used to support a claim.

Evidence that is out of date must be revisited to decide if there is more up-to-date information. Specifically, statistics and small research projects may have been refuted following the publication. You can find marketing materials from the 1930's stating that cigarettes are "physician approved" and suggested to be good for your health. Comparing this to a more recent study will provide more specific evidence as to why this claim is not true.

An author's credentials can also be analyzed. For example, a webpage from Wikipedia.com is often categorized as an unreliable source, whereas a webpage from a university library can be trusted. Peer reviewed academic articles typically include footnotes that provide the sources used to make their claims, the date they were written, and the name of the author. Quickly skimming an article for dates and names of sources will give a reader a better idea of the credibility of the evidence used.

College Composition
Sample Test

There are 50 questions that you must answer in less than 50 minutes. Then, there are essay questions that you must answer in a timed fashion: the first essay has 30 minutes and the second essay has 40 minutes to read two passages and complete and essay.

Remember, your goals for this test are those questions you answer accurately; it is not based on how many are incorrect. Take your time, and good luck.

Conventions of Standard Written English

Directions: Read each item carefully, paying attention to the underlined portions. If there is an error, it will be underlined. Assume that elements of the sentence not underlined are correct. If there is an error, select the one underlined part and enter that letter on the answer sheet. If there is no error, choose E

1. On a long day in October, the rain <u>fell</u> so hard that it <u>causes</u> flooding all <u>along</u> the highway, <u>bringing</u> traffic to a stop. <u>No error.</u>

    (A) fell

    (B) causes

    (C) along

    (D) bringing

    (E) No error

2. <u>Their</u> attempts are almost always comical, not <u>being able</u> to move supplies without <u>loosing</u> at least one package on the <u>route</u>. <u>No error</u>.

(A) Their

(B) being able

(C) loosing

(D) route

(E) No error

3. At least two of the seven <u>defendents</u> <u>want</u> a delay, <u>saying</u> they need more time <u>to prepare</u> for trial. <u>No error</u>.

(A) defendents

(B) want

(C) saying

(D) to prepare

(E) No error

4. The surfer <u>was bit</u> by a shark, but <u>got</u> his revenge when he <u>caught</u> him and <u>ate</u> it for dinner. <u>No error</u>.

(A) was bit

(B) got

(C) caught

(D) ate

(E) No error

5. A portrait of a <u>women</u> <u>had been</u> painted onto an iceberg, which was precariously <u>perched</u> on the edge of a melting <u>piece</u> of glacier. <u>No error</u>.

(A) women

(B) had been

(C) perched

(D) piece

(E) No error

Revision Skills

Read the following paragraph and answer the questions that follow.

There was a steaming mist in all the hollows, and it roamed in its forlornness up the hill, like an evil spirit, seeking rest and finding none. A clammy and intensely cold mist, it made its way through the air in ripples that visibly followed and overspread one another, as the waves of an unwholesome sea might do. It was dense enough to shut out everything from the light of the coach-lamps but these its own workings, and a few yards of road; and the reek of the laboring horses steamed into it, as if they had made it at all.

6. **The description of this scene gives the impression that it is:**

(A) an oppressive journey.

(B) an enlightening route.

(C) a contemplative traveling discussion.

(D) an entertaining troupe making way to the next show.

(E) None of these things is true.

7. **What is the main idea of this passage?**

   (A) Weather sets the stage in any narrative.

   (B) The coach horses were not up to the task of the road.

   (C) It was a dark and cold night, relatively unsuitable for travel.

   (D) One of the coach-lamps was unlit, making it difficult to see.

   (E) An English countryside scene is perfect for a scary setting.

8. **The author's purpose is to:**

   (A) Inform

   (B) Entertain

   (C) Persuade

   (D) Narrate

   (E) Analyze

Read the following passage and answer the questions that follow.

Everyone called him Pop Eye. Even in those days when I was a skinny thirteen-year-old I thought he probably knew about his nickname but didn't care. His eyes were too interested in what lay up ahead to notice us barefoot kids.

He looked like someone who had seen or known great suffering and hadn't been able to forget it. His large eyes in his large head stuck out further than anyone else's - like they wanted to lave the surface of his face. They made you think of someone who can't get out the house quickly enough.

Pop Eye wore the same white linen suit every day. His trousers snagged onto his bony knees in the sloppy heat. Some days he wore a clown's nose. His nose was already big. He didn't need that red light bulb. But for reasons we couldn't think of he wore the red nose on certain days that may have meant something to him. We never saw him smile. And on those days he wore the clowns nose you found yourself looking away because you never saw such sadness.

9. **What is the main idea of the passage?**

   (A) The main character was a generally sad man, disinterested in the scene around him.

   (B) The main character cannot remember the thirteen-year-old kid.

   (C) The physical appearance of the main character was awkward.

   (D) The main character was so poor that he only had one suit.

   (E) None of these represent the main idea of the passage.

10. **From the passage, one can infer that:**

   (A) Pop Eye is surrounded by family.

   (B) Pop Eye works as a clown.

   (C) The narrator is related to Pop Eye.

   (D) Pop Eye lives a lonely life.

   (E) The narrator has done well for himself.

11. **What is the author's purpose in writing this passage?**

   (A) To entertain

   (B) To narrate

   (C) To describe

   (D) To persuade

   (E) To make demands

12. **The author implies that :**

   (A) the main character had secret talents.

   (B) the main character had great sadness.

   (C) the narrator was related to the main character.

   (D) the main character was generally neat and tidy.

   (E) the narrator was homeless.

Read the following passage excerpted from Biography.com and choose the best answer to the questions that follow.

A prolific artist, Austrian composer Wolfgang Mozart created a string of operas, concertos, symphonies and sonatas that profoundly shaped classical music. Over the years, Mozart aligned himself with a variety of European venues and patrons, composing hundreds of works that included sonatas, symphonies, masses, concertos and operas, marked by vivid emotion and sophisticated textures.

During the time when he worked for Archbishop Hieronymus von Colleredo, young Mozart had the opportunity to work in several different musical genres composing symphonies, string quartets, sonatas and serenades and a few operas. He developed a passion for violin concertos producing what came to be the only five he wrote. In 1776, he turned his efforts toward piano concertos, culminating in the Piano Concerto Number 9 in E flat major in early 1777. In Salzburg in 1779, Wolfgang Amadeus Mozart produced a series of church works, including the Coronation Mass. He also composed another opera for Munich, Ideomeneo in 1781.

13. **Who is the target audience of this passage?**

   (A) Artists.

   (B) Austrians.

   (C) Catholics.

   (D) A person interested in classical music.

   (E) None of these are accurate.

14. **What is the main idea of the previous passage?**

   (A) Mozart had a sister that also performed with him.

   (B) Mozart's father was his promoter.

   (C) The Catholic church was supportive of Mozart's talent.

   (D) Many operas and other pieces were composed by Mozart before he was 25 years old.

   (E) The rapid development and appreciation of Mozart's music.

15. **What is the author's purpose in writing this?**

   (A) To describe

   (B) To narrate

   (C) To entertain

   (D) To inform

   (E) To argue

16. **From reading this passage, we can conclude that:**

   (A) Mozart wrote several complex pieces of music at a young age.

   (B) There were not many composers as young and talented as Mozart.

   (C) There was a special relationship between the Catholic church and Mozart's family.

   (D) There were not as many composers in Austria as other countries.

   (E) None of these are accurate.

17. **Which of the following is not a musical genre?**

   (A) Opera

   (B) Sonnet

   (C) Symphony.

   (D) Concerto.

   (E) Quartet.

Read the following paragraph and answer the questions that follow.

(1) Outside, the late afternoon sun slanted down in the yard, throwing into gleaming brightness the dogwood trees that were solid masses of white blossoms against the background of new green.

(2) The twins' horses were hitched in the driveway, big animals, red as their masters' hair; and around the horses' legs quarreled the pack of lean, nervous possum hounds that accompanied Stuart and Brent wherever they went

(3) A little aloof, as became and aristocrat, lay a black-spotted carriage dog, puzzle on paws, patiently waiting for the boys to go home to supper.

18. What is the main idea of this passage?

(A) The passage is describing an afternoon outdoor setting.

(B) The twins had very poised animals.

(C) Certain concessions should be made for dogs.

(D) The difficulties of travel in thick blossoming forests.

(E) None of these covey the main idea of the passage.

19. What is the author's main purpose?

(A) To inform

(B) To entertain

(C) To describe

(D) To narrate

(E) To record

20. What type of sentence is the second sentence?

(A) Simple

(B) Compound

(C) Complex

(D) Complex-Compound

(E) Dependent clause

Read the following paragraph from Wikipedia and answer the question that follows.

Isaac Newton built the first practical reflecting telescope and developed a theory of colour based on the observation that a prism decomposes white light into the many colors of the visible spectrum. He formulated an empirical law of cooling, studied the speed of sound, and introduced the notion of a Newtonian fluid. In addition to his work on calculus, as a mathematician Newton contributed to the study of power series, generalized the binomial theorem to non-integer exponents, developed a method for approximating the roots of a function, and classified most of the cubic plane curves.

21. What is the main idea of this passage?

(A) Power series is an important part of scientific discovery.

(B) Fluid engineering is about the empirical law of cooling.

(C) Through telescopes, scientists have made discoveries that have helped many people.

(D) Newton was a mathematician and a scientist.

(E) None of the above.

Read the following paragraph from *Popular Mechanics* and answer the question that follows.

We've been finding planets beyond our solar system for two decades now, but there are good reasons why it's taken so long to find the first forming world. For one thing, Stephanie Sallum says, planets spend only a brief period of their long lives in formation. Simply looking at the the odds, "it's unlikely that you'll come across a planet when it's still forming," she says.

22. The author's purpose is to

(A) Describe

(B) Inform

(C) Persuade

(D) Narrate

(E) Summarize

Read the following paragraph from *National Geographic* and answer the question.

So far, more than 150 countries – from Sudan to Suriname and from Kiribati to Kyrgyzstan – have outlined for United Nations negotiators just how, when, and by how much each would cut carbon dioxide over the next several decades. If an agreement is reached, it would mark the first serious global commitment to reduce the pollution that is warming the planet, souring the oceans, and causing seas to rise.

23. What type of organizational pattern is the author using?

(A) Comparison and Contrast

(B) Generalization

(C) Cause and Effect

(D) Simple Listing

(E) Analogy

Read the following paragraph from *Antiques and Fine Art* and answer the following question.

Since the colonial period, the Atlantic Ocean has operated both as a barrier between America and Europe and as a conduit for international exchanges of peoples, goods, and ideas. It spurred commerce and enterprise that was the basis for both national economic activity and personal fortune. The activities in America's great harbors and port cities also supported the nation's cultural development, prompting the rise of schools of maritime and landscape painting, as well as portraiture.

24. Which organizational pattern does the author use?

(A) Comparison and Contrast

(B) Simple Listing

(C) Cause and Effect

(D) Definition

(E) Description

Read the following quote and answer the following question.

"I don't think about whether people will remember me or not. I've been an okay person. I've learned a lot. I've taught people a thing or two. That's what's important." – Julia Child

25. The quote primarily:

(A) describes.

(B) informs.

(C) entertains.

(D) narrates.

(E) lists.

26. Addressing someone absent or something inhuman as though present and able to respond describes a figure of speech known as:

(A) personification

(B) synecdoche

(C) metonymy

(D) apostrophe

(E) rhetorical strategy

Ability to Use Source Material

Read the following paragraphs and answer the questions that follows.

At the end of the period, the artistic temperament of the painter undergoes a profound modification; it reflects a set of assimilated romantic ideas, expands the grandeur of classical art, and, while in the early works the love for the antique style throughout the popular subjects with inanimate edifice with the classic treatment as well as characterless, mythological subjects in the frescoes. The painter's figures assume heroic proportions, exude solemn expressions, and everything seems to come alive in a life more lush, more monumental and simple at the same time...

Overall, we find an artist's determined personality, animated by a continuous and rapid progress, the result of a clear conscience and scrupulous study fiery aspects of reality with which can be sympathized, of an intense search of technical development, the assimilation of many and beautiful expressions of art. So he states, from the beginning of his artistic activity, a teacher of exceptional importance, which rises with noble means and personal and solid, without resorting to defiant rage, the glitz, the stylism that characterize so remarkable part of the art of his time.

Serra, Luigi. Domenico Zampieri detto Il Domenichino. Rome: Casa Editrice del Bollettino d'Arte, Del Ministero Della P. Istruzione. 1909. pp11-12.

27. Where does the excerpt originate?

   (A) Webster's Dictionary

   (B) Luigi Serra

   (C) Domenico Zampieri

   (D) World Book Encyclopedia

   (E) Wikipedia

28. In the second paragraph, the second sentence can best be described as:

   (A) compound.

   (B) complex.

   (C) run-on.

   (D) a fragment.

   (E) compound-complex.

29. This, H. (2006). Food for Tomorrow? How the Scientific Discipline of Molecular Gastronomy Could Change the Way We Eat. *EMBO Reports*, 7(11), 1062-1066.

In the citation, 1062 provides what information?

(A) Date printed

(B) Date accessed

(C) First page of reference

(D) Last page of reference

(E) None of these are correct

30. In the citation above, the (11) refers to:

(A) the eleventh article in the magazine.

(B) the eleventh article published by this author.

(C) there are eleven articles on gastronomy in this issue.

(D) there are eleven authors.

(E) This is the eleventh issue in the series, in volume seven.

31. In the *EMBO* citation above, 7 refers to what?

(A) The number of volumes this has magazine has published in 2006.

(B) How many articles have discussed gastronomy in the magazine's history

(C) The seventh report for this issue.

(D) Pagination.

(E) Tagnemics

32. **Bernstein, M. (2002). 10 tips on writing the living Web.** *A List Apart: For People Who Make Websites*, **149. Retrieved from http://www.alistapart.com/articles/writeliving is a citation example of a:**

(A) newspaper.

(B) book.

(C) online periodical.

(D) abstract.

(E) none of these selections are accurate.

33. **2. Weinstein, "Plato's** *Republic*,**" 452–53.**

   This is an example of:

(A) note style.

(B) duplicate style.

(C) bibliography.

(D) APA style.

(E) MLA style.

34. **Kossinets, Gueorgi, and Duncan J. Watts. "Origins of Homophily in an Evolving Social Network."** *American Journal of Sociology* **115 (2009): 405–50. Accessed February 28, 2010. doi:10.1086/599247.**

   Which style is this?

(A) MLA

(B) APA

(C) Chicago

(D) New York

(E) None of these

35. Maxmen, Amy. "How Ebola Found Fertile Ground in Sierra Leone's Chaotic Capital." *National Geographic.* 27 January, 2015. Web. 16 November, 2015.

This is an example of what kind of citation format?

(A) MLA

(B) APA

(C) Chicago

(D) Turabian

(E) None of these

36. In the citation above, what does 27 January 2015 reference?

(A) Reference date

(B) Publication date

(C) Editing date

(D) Web upload date

(E) None of these

37. Treverton, Gregory F. "The Changed Target." *Intelligence for an Age of Terror.* Cambridge: Cambridge UP, 2009. 24-25. Print. What does print reference?

(A) Magazine article

(B) Newspaper article

(C) Printed web source

(D) Book

(E) None of these

Rhetorical Analysis

Read the following paragraph from the *National Independent Schools Magazine* and answer the questions that follow.

The bias against introverted students is embedded in our educational system: years of unrelenting focus on cooperative learning, thinking aloud, and talking-as-learning, with grades for class participation, required public speaking (often now as a disproportionate pedagogical focus displacing more traditional forms of scholarship and substantive mastery), and a pervasive, almost normative, value placed on being social and well liked, particularly in a large-group context. In sum, the classroom focus is now too often on "doing," in sacrifice to "thinking."

38. What is meant by the word "unrelenting" in the first sentence?

(A) Continuing

(B) Protective

(C) Pervasive

(D) Cautious

(E) Reckless

39. What is the author's tone?

(A) Aseptic

(B) Analytical

(C) Disbelieving

(D) Disapproving

(E) Scornful

40. What type of organizational pattern is the author using?

(A) Classification

(B) Explanation

(C) Comparison and Contrast

(D) Cause and Effect

(E) Entertaining

41. Who would be the intended audience of this excerpt?

(A) Politicians, for funding purposes.

(B) Social workers, for counseling purposes.

(C) Teachers, for refocusing efforts.

(D) Parents, for normative adjustments.

(E) None of these are applicable.

Read the following passage from *Roll of Thunder, Hear My Cry* and answer the questions that follow.

My youngest brother paid no attention to me. Grasping more firmly his newspaper-wrapped notebook and his tin-can lunch of cornbread and oil sausages, he continued to concentrate on the dusty road. He lagged several feet behind my other brothers, Stacey and Christopher-John, and me, attempting to keep the rusty Mississippi dust from swelling with each step and drifting back upon his shiny black shoes and the cuffs of his corduroy pants by lifting each foot high before setting it gently down again. Always meticulously neat, six-year-old Little Man never allowed dirt or tears or stains to mar anything he owned. Today was no exception.

"You keep it up and make us late for school, Mama's gonna wear you out," I threatened, pulling with exasperation at the high collar of the Sunday dress Mama had made me wear for the first day of school - as if that event were something special. It seemed to me that showing up at school all on a bright August-like October morning made for running the cool forest trails and wading barefoot in the forest pond was concession enough; Sunday clothing was asking too much. Christopher-John and Stacey were not too pleased about the clothing or school either. Only Little Man, just beginning his school career, found the prospects of both intriguing.

42. What is the meaning of the word "meticulously" in the next to last sentence in the first paragraph?

(A) Many

(B) Very

(C) Exceptionally

(D) Rarely

(E) Fairly

43. What is the overall organizational pattern used in this passage?

(A) Generalization

(B) Cause and Effect

(C) Addition

(D) Descriptive

(E) Informational

44. What is the author's tone?

(A) Disbelieving

(B) Exasperated

(C) Informative

(D) Optimistic

(E) None of these are correct.

Read the following passage from Pride and Prejudice and answer the questions that follow.

Mr. Bennet was so odd a mixture of quick parts, sarcastic humour, reserve, and caprice, that the experience of three-and-twenty years had been insufficient to make his wife understand his character. Her mind was less difficult to develop. She was a woman of mean understanding, little information, and uncertain temper. When she was discontented, she fancied herself nervous. The business of her life was to get her daughters married; its solace was visiting and news.

Mr. Bennet was among the earliest of those who waited on Mr. Bingley. He had always intended to visit him, though to the last always assuring his wife that he should not go; and till the evening after the visit was paid she had no knowledge of it. It was then disclosed in the following manner. Observing his second daughter employed in trimming a hat, he suddenly addressed her with:

"I hope Mr. Bingley will like it, Lizzy."

45. What is the overall organizational pattern of this passage?

(A) Generalization

(B) Cause and Effect

(C) Addition

(D) Summary

(E) Informational

46. What is the meaning of the phrase "uncertain temper" in the third sentence?

(A) Hot tempered

(B) Quixotic emotions

(C) Unusually morose

(D) Generally happy

(E) None of these apply

47. What is the organizational pattern of the second paragraph?

(A) Cause and Effect

(B) Classification

(C) Addition

(D) Explanation

(E) None of these things

Read the following passage from Wuthering Heights and answer the questions that follow.

Before passing the threshold, I pause to admire a quantity of grotesque carving lavished over the front, and especially about the principal door; above which, among a wilderness of crumbling griffins and shameless little boys, I detected the date '1500,' and the name 'Hareton Earnshaw.' I would have made a few comments, and requested a short history of the plane from the surly owner; but his attitude at the door appeared to demand my speedy entrance, or complete departure, and I had no desire to aggregate his impatience previous to inspecting the penetralium.

48. What is the author's overall organizational pattern?

(A) Classification

(B) Cause and Effect

(C) Definition

(D) Comparison and Contrast

(E) None of these things

49. The author's tone in the passage is one of:

(A) Inquisition

(B) Excitement

(C) Surliness

(D) Concern

(E) Impatience

50. **The most similar way to rephrase "I had no desire to aggregate his impatience"in context of the passage would be:**

(A) I wanted to keep him happy

(B) I didn't want to make him mad

(C) I didn't want to stay around

(D) I wanted him to quickly inspect the penetralium

(E) None of these are approximations

Sample Test Essays

Readers will assign scores based on a matrix, or scoring guide. Here is an example outline of how both student essays will be graded on a six point scale.

SCORE OF 6: The 6 essay presents a thesis that is coherent and well-developed. The writer's ideas are detailed, intelligent, and thoroughly elaborated. The writer's use of language and structure is correct and meaningful.

SCORE OF 5: The 5 essay presents a thesis and offers persuasive support. The writer's ideas are usually new, mature, and thoroughly developed. A command of language and a variety of structures are evident.

SCORE OF 4: The 4 essay presents a thesis and frequently offers a plan of development, which is usually demonstrated. The writer offers sufficient details to achieve the purpose of the essay. There is capable use of language and varied sentence structure. Errors in sentence structure and usage don't interfere with the writer's main purpose.

SCORE OF 3: The 3 essay gives a thesis and offers a plan of development, which is usually demonstrated. The writer gives support that leans toward generalized statements or a listing. Overall, the support in a 3 essay is neither adequate nor coherent enough to be convincing. There are errors in sentence structure and usage that frequently interfere with the writer's ability to state the purpose.

SCORE OF 2: The 2 essay usually states a thesis. The writer offers support that may be incomplete. Simple and disconnected sentence structure is present. Mistakes in grammar and usage often thwart the writer's ability to state the purpose.

SCORE OF 1: The 1 essay has a thesis that is pointless or poorly articulated. Support is shallow. The language is muddled and confusing. Many mistakes in grammar and usage.

Essay 1

As a reminder, you have **30 minutes** to compose your essay and type it on the computer.

Directions: Write an essay in which you discuss the extent to which you agree or disagree with the statement below. Support your discussion with specific reasons and examples from your reading, experience or observations.

Topic: Beauty is in the eye of the beholder.

Essay 2

As a reminder, you have **40 minutes** to read these two passages and type your essay on the computer.

Directions: Write an essay in which you incorporate the two sources of information provided below. You must use both sources and you must use appropriate citation for both sources using the author's last name, the title or by any other means that adequately identifies it. Support your discussion with specific reasons and examples from your reading, experience or observations.

Assignment: Read the following sources carefully. Then write an essay in which you develop a position on whether people or communities express devotion differently.

Introduction: Devotion, according to Oxford's Dictionary, is "love, loyalty or enthusiasm for a person, activity, or cause."

Source 1: Shakespeare, William. *Romeo and Juliet.* England: 1595.

"But, soft! what light through yonder window breaks?
It is the east, and Juliet is the sun.
Arise, fair sun, and kill the envious moon,
Who is already sick and pale with grief,
That thou, her maid, art far more fair than she.
Be not her maid, since she is envious;
Her vestal livery is but sick and green
And none but fools do wear it; cast it off.

It is my lady, O, it is my love!
Oh, that she knew she were!"

Source 2: Heller, Joseph. "Catch 22." United States: 1961.
"What is a country? A country is a piece of land surrounded on all sides by boundaries, usually unnatural."

Composition Sample Test Answer Key _____

Sample Test One

Question Number	Correct Answer	Your Answer	Question Number	Correct Answer	Your Answer
1	B		26	A	
2	C		27	B	
3	A		28	C	
4	A		29	C	
5	A		30	E	
6	A		31	A	
7	C		32	C	
8	D		33	B	
9	A		34	C	
10	D		35	A	
11	C		36	B	
12	B		37	D	
13	D		38	A	
14	E		39	D	
15	D		40	D	
16	A		41	C	
17	B		42	C	
18	A		43	D	
19	C		44	B	
20	D		45	A	
21	D		46	B	
22	B		47	D	
23	C		48	E	
24	A		49	A	
25	B		50	B	

Conventions of Standard Written English

Directions: Read each item carefully, paying attention to the underlined portions. If there is an error, it will be underlined. Assume that elements of the sentence not underlined are correct. If there is an error, select the one underlined part and enter that letter on the answer sheet. If there is no error, choose E.

1. On a long day in October, the rain <u>fell</u> so hard that it <u>causes</u> flooding all <u>along</u> the highway, <u>bringing</u> traffic to a stop. <u>No error</u>.

   (A) fell

   (B) causes

   (C) along

   (D) bringing

   (E) No error

   The answer is B.
   Causes should be caused, as
   the sentence is written in the past tense.

2. <u>Their</u> attempts are almost always comical, not <u>being able</u> to move supplies without <u>loosing</u> at least one package on the <u>route</u>. <u>No error</u>.

   A Their

   (B) being able

   (C) loosing

   (D) route

   (E) No error

The answer is C.

The underlined word has one too many 'O's, and should be written as losing.

3. At least two of the seven <u>defendents</u> <u>want</u> a delay, <u>saying</u> they need more time <u>to prepare</u> for trial. <u>No error</u>.

    (A) defendents

    (B) want

    (C) saying

    (D) to prepare

    (E) No eror

The answer is A.

The word listed is misspelled frequently, and is correctly spelled defendants.

4. The surfer <u>was bit</u> by a shark, but <u>got</u> his revenge when he <u>caught</u> him and <u>ate</u> it for dinner. <u>No error</u>.

    (A) was bit

    (B) got

    (C) caught

    (D) ate

    (E) No error

The answer is A

as the appropriate past conjugation is was bitten.

5. A portrait of a <u>women</u> <u>had been</u> painted onto an iceberg, which was precariously <u>perched</u> on the edge of a melting <u>piece</u> of glacier. <u>No error.</u>

   (A) women

   (B) had been

   (C) perched

   (D) piece

   (E) No error

   The answer is A.

   The underlined word should be singular, woman, as indicated by the verb tense as well as the lead-in "a" (plural would be the).

Revision Skills

Read the following paragraph and answer the questions that follow.

There was a steaming mist in all the hollows, and it roamed in its forlornness up the hill, like an evil spirit, seeking rest and finding none. A clammy and intensely cold mist, it made its way through the air in ripples that visibly followed and overspread one another, as the waves of an unwholesome sea might do. It was dense enough to shut out everything from the light of the coach-lamps but these its own workings, and a few yards of road; and the reek of the laboring horses steamed into it, as if they had made it at all.

6. The description of this scene gives the impression that it is:

   (A) an oppressive journey.

   (B) an enlightening route.

   (C) a contemplative traveling discussion.

   (D) an entertaining troupe making way to the next show.

   (E) None of these things is true.

   The answer is A.

   Choice B is incorrect because there are no descriptive words that indicate "enlightening". C is incorrect as there is no discussion, and

D is also incorrect in that there is no reference whatsoever to justify this is true.

7. **What is the main idea of this passage?**

   (A) Weather sets the stage in any narrative.

   (B) The coach horses were not up to the task of the road.

   (C) It was a dark and cold night, relatively unsuitable for travel.

   (D) One of the coach-lamps was unlit, making it difficult to see.

   (E) An English countryside scene is perfect for a scary setting.

   The answer is C.

   While all options may be true, the only one that is correct on a high level without excluding other pieces of the narrative makes C the best answer.

8. **The author's purpose is to:**

   (A) Inform

   (B) Entertain

   (C) Persuade

   (D) Narrate

   (E) Analyze

   The answer is D.

   The author is simply narrating the setting for the action of the plot.

Read the following passage and answer the questions that follow.

Everyone called him Pop Eye. Even in those days when I was a skinny thirteen-year-old I thought he probably knew about his nickname but didn't care. His eyes were too interested in what lay up ahead to notice us barefoot kids.

He looked like someone who had seen or known great suffering and hadn't been able to forget it. His large eyes in his large head stuck out further than anyone else's - like they wanted to lave the surface of his face. They made you think of someone who can't get out the house quickly enough.

Pop Eye wore the same white linen suit every day. His trousers snagged onto his bony knees in the sloppy heat. Some days he wore a clown's nose. His nose was already big. He didn't need that red light bulb. But for reasons we couldn't think of he wore the red nose on certain days that may have meant something to him. We never saw him smile. And on those days he wore the clowns nose you found yourself looking away because you never saw such sadness.

9. **What is the main idea of the passage?**

   (A) The main character was a generally sad man, disinterested in the scene around him.

   (B) The main character cannot remember the thirteen-year-old kid

   (C) The physical appearance of the main character was awkward.

   (D) The main character was so poor that he only had one suit.

   (E) None of these represent the main idea of the passage.

   The answer is A.
   While options B through D are correct according to the passage, the overall idea is encompassed in A.

10. **From the passage, one can infer that:**

   (A) Pop Eye is surrounded by family.

   (B) Pop Eye works as a clown.

   (C) The narrator is related to Pop Eye.

   (D) Pop Eye lives a lonely life.

   (E) The narrator has done well for himself.

The answer is D.

No other options are supported by information in the passage.

11. What is the author's purpose in writing this passage?

(A) To entertain

(B) To narrate

(C) To describe

(D) To persuade

(E) To make demands

The answer is C.

The author does describe the scene more than any other options. The author sets the scene for future plot development.

12. The author implies that:

(A) the main character had secret talents.

(B) the main character had great sadness.

(C) the narrator was related to the main character.

(D) the main character was generally neat and tidy.

(E) the narrator was homeless.

The answer is B.

This fact is directly stated in the last paragraph.

Read the following passage excerpted from Biography.com and choose the best answer to the questions that follow.

A prolific artist, Austrian composer Wolfgang Mozart created a string of operas, concertos, symphonies and sonatas that profoundly shaped classical music. Over the years, Mozart aligned himself with a variety of European venues and patrons, composing hundreds of works that included sonatas, symphonies, masses, concertos and operas, marked by vivid emotion and sophisticated textures.

During the time when he worked for Archbishop Hieronymus von Colleredo, young Mozart had the opportunity to work in several different musical genres composing symphonies, string quartets, sonatas and serenades and a few operas. He developed a passion for violin concertos producing what came to be the only five he wrote. In 1776, he turned his efforts toward piano concertos, culminating in the Piano Concerto Number 9 in E flat major in early 1777. In Salzburg in 1779, Wolfgang Amadeus Mozart produced a series of church works, including the Coronation Mass. He also composed another opera for Munich, Ideomeneo in 1781.

13. Who is the target audience of this passage?

(A) Artists.

(B) Austrians.

(C) Catholics.

(D) A person interested in classical music.

(E) None of these are accurate.

The answer is D.

While the other options use listed words in the selection, the answer most correct is D.

Sample Test One   79

14. What is the main idea of the previous passage?

(A) Mozart had a sister that also performed with him.

(B) Mozart's father was his promoter.

(C) The Catholic church was supportive of Mozart's talent.

(D) Many operas and other pieces were composed by Mozart before he was 25 years old.

(E) The rapid development and appreciation of Mozart's music.

The answer is E.

While all of the items are facts and listed in the context of the passage, the overall main idea is expressed in E.

15. What is the author's purpose in writing this?

(A) To describe

(B) To narrate

(C) To entertain

(D) To inform

(E) To argue

The answer is D.

The author is providing the reader with information about musicality and progress of Mozart's development.

16. From reading this passage, we can conclude that:

(A) Mozart wrote several complex pieces of music at a young age.

(B) There were not many composers as young and talented as Mozart.

(C) There was a special relationship between the Catholic church and Mozart's family.

(D) There were not as many composers in Austria as other countries.

(E) None of these are accurate.

The answer is A.

Options B through D express opinions not supported in the passage.

17. Which of the following is not a musical genre?

(A) Opera

(B) Sonnet

(C) Symphony.

(D) Concerto.

(E) Quartet.

The answer is B.

A Sonnet is a poem form while a Sonota is a musical form. This correct form is directly listed in the passage.

Read the following paragraph and answer the questions that follow.

(1)Outside, the late afternoon sun slanted down in the yard, throwing into gleaming brightness the dogwood trees that were solid masses of white blossoms against the background of new green. (2)The twins' horses were hitched in the driveway, big animals, red as their masters' hair; and around the horses' legs quarreled the pack of lean, nervous possum hounds that accompanied Stuart and Brent wherever they went. (3)A little aloof, as became and aristocrat, lay a black-spotted carriage dog, puzzle on paws, patiently waiting for the boys to go home to supper.

18. What is the main idea of this passage?

(A) The passage is describing an afternoon outdoor setting.

(B) The twins had very poised animals.

(C) Certain concessions should be made for dogs.

(D) The difficulties of travel in thick blossoming forests.

(E) None of these covey the main idea of the passage.

The answer is A.

Option B is not true, as the dogs were quarreling around the horses' legs; Option C is not conveyed in the passage; Option D is not relayed in the passage anywhere about the group traveling.

19. What is the author's main purpose?

(A) To inform

(B) To entertain

(C) To describe

(D) To narrate

(E) To record

The answer is C.
The author is simply describing the scene.

20. What type of sentence is the second sentence?

(A) Simple

(B) Compound

(C) Complex

(D) Complex-Compound

(E) Dependent clause

The answer is D.
A semi-colon is even used, which is typical to conjoin to complex sentences. With the use of conjunctions (and), this also makes it compound.

Read the following paragraph from Wikipedia and answer the question that follows.

Isaac Newton built the first practical reflecting telescope and developed a theory of colour based on the observation that a prism decomposes white light into the many colors of the visible spectrum. He formulated an empirical law of cooling, studied the speed of sound, and introduced the notion of a Newtonian fluid. In addition to his work on calculus, as a mathematician Newton contributedto the study of power series, generalized the binomial theorem to non-integer exponents, developed a method for approximating the roots of a function, and classified most of the cubic plane curves.

21. What is the main idea of this passage?

(A) Power series is an important part of scientific discovery.

(B) Fluid engineering is about the empirical law of cooling.

(C) Through telescopes, scientists have made discoveries that have helped many people.

(D) Newton was a mathematician and a scientist.

(E) None of the above.

The answer is D.
While the first three options are correct, the fourth gives a higher-level viewpoint of the overall passage.

Read the following paragraph from *Popular Mechanics* and answer the question that follows.

We've been finding planets beyond our solar system for two decades now, but there are good reasons why it's taken so long to find the first forming world. For one thing, Stephanie Sallum says, planets spend only a brief period of their long lives in formation. Simply looking at the the the odds, "it's unlikely that you'll come across a planet when it's still forming," she says.

22. The author's purpose is to

(A) Describe

(B) Inform

(C) Persuade

(D) Narrate

(E) Summarize

The answer is B.
Option B is correct in that the discussion is about the new discovery of plants and the reasons that it has been hard to discover.

Read the following paragraph from *National Geographic* and answer the question.

So far, more than 150 countries – from Sudan to Suriname and from Kiribati to Kyrgyzstan – have outlined for United Nations negotiators just how, when, and by how much each would cut carbon dioxide over the next several decades. If an agreement is reached, it would mark the first serious global commitment to reduce the pollution that is warming the planet, souring the oceans, and causing seas to rise.

23. What type of organizational pattern is the author using?

(A) Comparison and Contrast

(B) Generalization

(C) Cause and Effect

(D) Simple Listing

(E) Analogy

The answer is C.

The author lists some causes and effects for fighting global warming.

Read the following paragraph from *Antiques and Fine Art* and answer the following question.

Since the colonial period, the Atlantic Ocean has operated both as a barrier between America and Europe and as a conduit for international exchanges of peoples, goods, and ideas. It spurred commerce and enterprise that was the basis for both national economic activity and personal fortune. The activities in America's great harbors and port cities also supported the nation's cultural development, prompting the rise of schools of maritime and landscape painting, as well as portraiture.

24. Which organizational pattern does the author use?

(A) Comparison and Contrast

(B) Simple Listing

(C) Cause and Effect

(D) Definition

(E) Description

The answer is A.

Since the author is demonstrating differences between America and Europe around the Atlantic Ocean, the correct answer is (A).

Read the following quote and answer the following question.

"I don't think about whether people will remember me or not. I've been an okay person. I've learned a lot. I've taught people a thing or two. That's what's important." – Julia Child

25. The quote primarily:

(A) describes.

(B) informs.

(C) entertains.

(D) narrates.

(E) lists.

The answer is B.

Since the quote telling us how Julia Child saw her life, the correct answer here is (B).

26. **Addressing someone absent or something inhuman as though present and able to respond describes a figure of speech known as:**

   (A) personification

   (B) synecdoche

   (C) metonymy

   (D) apostrophe

   (E) rhetorical strategy

   The answer is A.

   Personification is taking something inhuman and giving it personal traits (such as responding).

Ability to Use Source Material

Read the following paragraphs and answer the questions that follows.

At the end of the period, the artistic temperament of the painter undergoes a profound modification; it reflects a set of assimilated romantic ideas, expands the grandeur of classical art, and, while in the early works the love for the antique style throughout the popular subjects with inanimate edifice with the classic treatment as well as characterless, mythological subjects in the frescoes. The painter's figures assume heroic proportions, exude solemn expressions, and everything seems to come alive in a life more lush, more monumental and simple at the same time…

Overall, we find an artist's determined personality, animated by a continuous and rapid progress, the result of a clear conscience and scrupulous study fiery aspects of reality with which can be sympathized, of an intense search of technical development, the assimilation of many and beautiful expressions of art. So he states, from the beginning of his artistic activity, a teacher of exceptional importance, which rises with noble means and personal and solid, without resorting to defiant rage, the glitz, the stylism that characterize so remarkable part of the art of his time.

Serra, Luigi. Domenico Zampieri detto Il Domenichino.Rome: Casa Editrice del Bollettino d'Arte, Del Ministero Della P. Istruzione. 1909. pp11-12.

27. Where does the excerpt originate?

(A) Webster's Dictionary

(B) Luigi Serra

(C) Domenico Zampieri

(D) World Book Encyclopedia

(E) Wikipedia

The answer is B.

It is listed as the source directly below the passage, and in the format, Serra is the author. Zampieri is the subject of the material.

28. In the second paragraph, the second sentence can best be described as:

(A) compound.

(B) complex.

(C) run-on.

(D) a fragment.

(E) compound-complex.

The answer is C

which is just a fact that you need to know when answering questions in this section.

29. This, H. (2006). Food for Tomorrow? How the Scientific Discipline of Molecular Gastronomy Could Change the Way We Eat. *EMBO Reports,* 7(11), 1062-1066.

In the citation, 1062 provides what information?

(A) Date printed

(B) Date accessed

(C) First page of reference *

(D) Last page of reference

(E) None of these are correct

The answer is C.

The first page of the reference cited.

30. In the citation above, the (11) refers to:

(A) the eleventh article in the magazine.

(B) the eleventh article published by this author.

(C) there are eleven articles on gastronomy in this issue.

(D) there are eleven authors.

(E) This is the eleventh issue in the series, in volume seven.

The answer is E.

The citation for the correct issue in the correctly listed volume.

31. In the *EMBO* citation above, 7 refers to what?

(A) The number of volumes this has magazine has published in 2006

(B) How many articles have discussed gastronomy in the magazine's history

(C) The seventh report for this issue

(D) Pagination

(E) Tagnemics

The answer is A

as it lists the correct volume from the original citation.

32. Bernstein, M. (2002). 10 tips on writing the living Web. *A List Apart: For People Who Make Websites*, 149. Retrieved from http://www.alistapart.com/articles/writeliving is a citation example of a:

(A) newspaper.

(B) book.

(C) online periodical.

(D) abstract.

(E) none of these selections are accurate.

The answer is C.

Option C is correct, which should be evident not only by the title but also the website listed in the citation.

33. 2. Weinstein, "Plato's *Republic*," 452–53.

This is an example of:

(A) note style.

(B) duplicate style.

(C) bibliography.

(D) APA style.

(E) MLA style.

The answer is B

as if it was any of the others, it would have a complete first and last name as well as place of publication and year.

34. **Kossinets, Gueorgi, and Duncan J. Watts. "Origins of Homophily in an Evolving Social Network."** *American Journal of Sociology* **115 (2009): 405–50. Accessed February 28, 2010. doi:10.1086/599247.**

    Which style is this?

    (A) MLA

    (B) APA

    (C) Chicago

    (D) New York

    (E) None of these

    The answer is C.

    The year comes later in Chicago format and the second name is listed in first name last name order.

35. **Maxmen, Amy. "How Ebola Found Fertile Ground in Sierra Leone's Chaotic Capital."** *National Geographic.* **27 January, 2015. Web. 16 November, 2015.**

    This is an example of what kind of citation format?

    (A) MLA

    (B) APA

    (C) Chicago

    (D) Turabian

    (E) None of these

    The answer is A

    as this is MLA citation format. These are facts, the differences between citation types that should be known for the test.

36. In the citation above, what does 27 January 2015 reference?

(A) Reference date

(B) Publication date

(C) Editing date

(D) Web upload date

(E) None of these

The answer is B

as this is the publication date. The reference date comes at the end. Any editing or version dates would come after the title with an editor's name.

37. Treverton, Gregory F. "The Changed Target." *Intelligence for an Age of Terror.* **Cambridge: Cambridge UP, 2009. 24-25. Print. What does print reference?**

(A) Magazine article

(B) Newspaper article

(C) Printed web source

(D) Book

(E) None of these

The answer is D.

The "print" gives that fact.

Rhetorical Analysis

Read the following paragraph from the *National Independent Schools Magazine* **and answer the questions that follow.**

The bias against introverted students is embedded in our educational system: years of unrelenting focus on cooperative learning, thinking aloud, and talking-as-learning, with grades for class participation, required public speaking (often now as a disproportionate pedagogical focus displacing more traditional forms of scholarship and substantive mastery), and a pervasive, almost normative, value placed on being social and well liked, particularly in a large-group context. In sum, the classroom focus is now too often on "doing," in sacrifice to "thinking."

38. What is meant by the word "unrelenting" in the first sentence?

(A) Continuing

(B) Protective

(C) Pervasive

(D) Cautious

(E) Reckless

The answer is A

and should be able to be determined through careful reading of the passage. This is a key to succeeding in this section, being able to analyze and replace words with similar meanings.

39. What is the author's tone?

(A) Aseptic

(B) Analytical

(C) Disbelieving

(D) Disapproving

(E) Scornful

The answer is D.

The author uses words that show disapproval of bias against introverted students throughout the passage.

40. What type of organizational pattern is the author using?

(A) Classification

(B) Explanation

(C) Comparison and Contrast

(D) Cause and Effect

(E) Entertaining

The answer is D.

The author mentions the things that are being pushed onto children that may not learn best in that style and has clearly stated "bias against" - this would be most correctly listed as effect and cause, but is the best option as it is not typical to list "effect and cause" in choices.

41. Who would be the intended audience of this excerpt?

(A) Politicians, for funding purposes.

(B) Social workers, for counseling purposes.

(C) Teachers, for refocusing efforts.

(D) Parents, for normative adjustments.

(E) None of these are applicable.

The answer is C.

There is no mention of funding or politics; there is no mention of social workers or counseling; there is no mention of parents or adjustments. Though any of these groups and purposes may be targeted, we can only answer questions based on the information presented in the selections within the test. Be sure to not bring outside information into answering questions.

Read the following passage from *Roll of Thunder, Hear My Cry* and answer the questions that follow.

My youngest brother paid no attention to me. Grasping more firmly his newspaper-wrapped notebook and his tin-can lunch of cornbread and oil sausages, he continued to concentrate on the dusty road. He lagged several feet behind my other brothers, Stacey and Christopher-John, and me, attempting to keep the rusty Mississippi dust from swelling with each step and drifting back upon his shiny black shoes and the cuffs of his corduroy pants by lifting each foot high before setting it gently down again. Always meticulously neat, six-year-old Little Man never allowed dirt or tears or stains to mar anything he owned. Today was no exception.

"You keep it up and make us late for school, Mama's gonna wear you out," I threatened, pulling with exasperation at the high collar of the Sunday dress Mama had made me wear for the first day of school - as if that event were something special. It seemed to me that showing up at school all on a bright August-like October morning made for running the cool forest trails and wading barefoot in the forest pond was concession enough; Sunday clothing was asking too much. Christopher-John and Stacey were not too pleased about the clothing or school either. Only Little Man, just beginning his school career, found the prospects of both intriguing.

42. What is the meaning of the word "meticulously" in the next to last sentence in the first paragraph?

(A) Many

(B) Very

(C) Exceptionally

(D) Rarely

(E) Fairly

The answer is C.

While B and E may be correct, it is not emphatic enough and the other options are not applicable or opposite.

43. What is the overall organizational pattern used in this passage?

(A) Generalization

(B) Cause and Effect

(C) Addition

(D) Descriptive

(E) Informational

The answer is D.

The author describes the scene of the children walking down the dirt road.

44. What is the author's tone?

(A) Disbelieving

(B) Exasperated

(C) Informative

(D) Optimistic

(E) None of these are correct.

The answer is B.

The sister is the narrator for this passage and she actually uses the word "exasperation" in the first sentence of the second paragraph.

Read the following passage from Pride and Prejudice and answer the questions that follow.

Mr. Bennet was so odd a mixture of quick parts, sarcastic humour, reserve, and caprice, that the experience of three-and-twenty years had been insufficient to make his wife understand his character. Her mind was less difficult to develop. She was a woman of mean understanding, little information, and uncertain temper. When she was discontented, she fancied herself nervous. The business of her life was to get her daughters married; its solace was visiting and news.

Mr. Bennet was among the earliest of those who waited on Mr. Bingley. He had always intended to visit him, though to the last always assuring his wife that he should not go; and till the evening after the visit was paid she had no knowledge of it. It was then disclosed in the following manner. Observing his second daughter employed in trimming a hat, he suddenly addressed her with:

"I hope Mr. Bingley will like it, Lizzy."

45. What is the overall organizational pattern of this passage?

    (A) Generalization

    (B) Cause and Effect

    (C) Addition

    (D) Summary

    (E) Informational

The answer is A.

Because it was a description of the generalities with both Mr. as well as Mrs. Bennet. There is no cause and effect described, and C as well as D are not correct. E may be a tempting choice, but it is not relaying information - when data and facts (such as science) are given, that is when it's appropriate to select informational.

46. What is the meaning of the phrase "uncertain temper" in the third sentence?

(A) Hot tempered

(B) Quixotic emotions

(C) Unusually morose

(D) Generally happy

(E) None of these apply

The answer is B.

Answer A may seem a likely choice, except temper is not being used literally in this passage. C and D give one extreme or another, and that is not what is implied in the context of the passage either.

47. What is the organizational pattern of the second paragraph?

(A) Cause and Effect

(B) Classification

(C) Addition

(D) Explanation

(E) None of these things

The answer is D.

By selecting D, the explanation is how the second paragraph is organized, the reader shows that he or she understood that the narrator is providing explanation as to why Mr. Bennet didn't previously tell his wife about visiting Mr. Bingley and then why he did.

Read the following passage from Wuthering Heights and answer the questions that follow.

Before passing the threshold, I pause to admire a quantity of grotesque carving lavished over the front, and especially about the principal door; above which, among a wilderness of crumbling griffins and shameless little boys, I detected the date '1500,' and the name 'Hareton Earnshaw.' I would have made a few comments, and requested a short history of the plane from the surly owner; but his attitude at the door appeared to demand my speedy entrance, or complete departure, and I had no desire to aggregate his impatience previous to inspecting the penetralium.

48. What is the author's overall organizational pattern?

(A) Classification

(B) Cause and Effect

(C) Definition

(D) Comparison and Contrast

(E) None of these things

The answer is E.
The offered answers for organizational pattern of the passage are not correct; therefore, answer E is correct.

49. The author's tone in the passage is one of:

(A) Inquisition

(B) Excitement

(C) Surliness

(D) Concern

(E) Impatience

The answer is A.
The speaker actually says a few comments would have been made about what is seen in the room. Answer B is not conveyed in the passage. C, D, and E are words used to describe the male's attitude in the passage, so they could be immediately eliminated.

50. **The most similar way to rephrase "I had no desire to aggregate his impatience" in context of the passage would be:**

(A) I wanted to keep him happy

(B) I didn't want to make him mad

(C) I didn't want to stay around

(D) I wanted him to quickly inspect the penetralium

(E) None of these are approximations

The answer is B.

The correct rephrasing is B for most accurately representing a rephrased sentence. While A may be true from analysis, it is not correct syntax to match the phrase pulled from the passage. C and D are just not correct choices (D actually skips part of the sentence and tricks a reader moving too quickly by using the ending of the actual paragraph - make sure you read carefully!)

College Composition Modular Sample Test

Composition Modular Sample Test_____

Directions: Read each item carefully, paying attention to the underlined portions. If there is an error, it will be underlined. Assume that elements of the sentence not underlined are correct. If there is an error, select the one underlined part and enter that letter on the answer sheet. If there is no error, choose E.

1. A <u>fearful</u> man, all in grey, <u>were</u> down by the river <u>standing</u> by the bunches of <u>rushes</u>. <u>No error</u>.

    (A) fearful

    (B) were

    (C) standing

    (D) rushes

    (E) No error

2. When our group of <u>friends</u> goes to Italy next year, we will be <u>seeing</u> many of the <u>countries</u> famous <u>landmarks</u>. <u>No error</u>.

    (A) friends

    (B) seeing

    (C) countries

    (D) landmarks

    (E) No error

3. <u>Their</u> are no walls high enough, no <u>valleys</u> deep enough, <u>to</u> keep the warriors <u>from</u> attacking the city. <u>No error</u>.

    (A) Their

    (B) valleys

    (C) to

    (D) from

    (E) No error

4. <u>Whenever</u> the phone rings, the dog <u>likes</u> to run to the front door to <u>see</u> who <u>has come</u> to visit. <u>No error</u>.

(A) Whenever

(B) likes

(C) see

(D) has come

(E) No error

5. <u>Every one</u> must pass <u>through</u> Vanity Fair in order to get to the <u>celestial</u> city and receive <u>their</u> three golden eggs. <u>No error</u>

(A) Every one

(B) through

(C) celestial

(D) their

(E) No error

6. Suffering <u>has been</u> stronger than all other teaching, and <u>have</u> taught me to understand what <u>your</u> heart <u>use</u> to be. <u>No error</u>

(A) has been

(B) have

(C) your

(D) use

(E) No error

7. The loneliest moment in <u>someone's</u> life is when they are watching <u>their</u> <u>hole</u> world fall apart, and all they can do is <u>stare</u> blankly. <u>No error</u>

   (A) someone's

   (B) their

   (C) hole

   (D) stare

   (E) No error

8. I have not <u>broken</u> your heart - you have <u>broke</u> it; and in <u>breaking</u> it, you <u>have</u> broken mine. <u>No error</u>

   (A) broken

   (B) broke

   (C) breaking

   (D) have

   (E) No error

Read the following pragraph and answer the questions that follow.

Mr. Smith gave instructions for the painting to be hung on the wall. And then it leaped forth before his eyes: the little cottages on the river, the white clouds floating over the valley and the green of the towering mountain ranges which were seen in the distance. The painting was so vivid that it seemed almost real. Mr. Smith was now absolutely certain that the painting had been worth money.

9. From the last sentence, one can infer that:

   (A) the painting was expensive.

   (B) the painting was cheap.

   (C) Mr. Smith was considering purchasing the painting.

   (D) Mr. Smith thought the painting was too expensive and decided not to purchase it.

   (E) None of these things is true.

10. What is the main idea of this passage?

(A) The painting that Mr. Smith purchased is expensive.

(B) Mr. Smith purchased a painting.

(C) Mr. Smith was pleased with the quality of the painting he had purchased.

(D) The painting depicted cottages and valleys.

(E) Mr. Smith was looking to buy some paintings.

11. The author's purpose is to:

(A) Inform

(B) Entertain

(C) Persuade

(D) Narrate

(E) Analyze

Read the following passage and answer the questions that follow.

One of the most difficult problems plaguing American education is the assessment of teachers. No one denies that teachers ought to be answerable for what they do, but what exactly does that mean? The Oxford American Dictionary defines accountability as: the obligation to give a reckoning or explanation for one's actions.

Does a student have to learn for teaching to have taken place? Historically, teaching has not been defined in this restrictive manner; the teacher was thought to be responsible for the quantity and quality of material covered and the way in which it was presented. However, some definitions of teaching now imply that students must learn in order for teaching to have taken place.

As a teacher who tries my best to keep current on all the latest teaching strategies, I believe that those teachers who do not bother even to pick up an educational journal every once in a while should be kept under close watch. There are many teachers out there who have been teaching for decades and refuse to change their ways even if research has proven that their methods are outdated and ineffective. There is no place in the profession of teaching for these types of individuals. It is time that the American educational system clean house, for the sake of our children.

12. What is the main idea of the passage?

(A) Teachers should not be answerable for what they do.

(B) Teachers who do not do their job should be fired.

(C) The author is a good teacher.

(D) Assessment of teachers is a serious problem in society today.

(E) Defining accountability.

13. From the passage, one can infer that:

(A) The author considers herself a good teacher.

(B) Poor teachers will be fired.

(C) Students have to learn for teaching to take place.

(D) The author will be fired.

(E) All of these are characteristics of fables

14. What is the author's purpose in writing the passage on the previous page?

(A) To entertain

(B) To narrate

(C) To describe

(D) To persuade

(E) To make demands

15. The author states that teacher assessment is a problem for:

(A) Elementary schools

(B) Secondary schools

(C) American education

(D) Families

(E) Teachers

Read the following passage and answer the questions that follow.

Disciplinary practices have been found to affect diverse areas of child development such as the acquisition of moral values, obedience to authority, and performance at school. Even though the dictionary has a specific definition of the word "discipline," it is still open to interpretation by people of different cultures.

There are four types of disciplinary styles: assertion of power, withdrawal of love, reasoning, and permissiveness. Assertion of power involves the use of force to discourage unwanted behavior. Withdrawal of love involves making the love of a parent conditional on a child's good behavior. Reasoning involves persuading the child to behave one way rather than another. Permissiveness involves allowing the child to do as he or she pleases and face the consequences of his/her actions.

16. Name the four types of disciplinary styles.

(A) Reasoning, power assertion, morality, and permissiveness.

(B) Morality, reasoning, permissiveness, and withdrawal of love.

(C) Withdrawal of love, permissiveness, power, and reasoning.

(D) Permissiveness, morality, reasoning, and power assertion.

(E) Explore, Inform, Entertain, Persuade.

17. What is the main idea of the previous passage?

(A) Different people have different ideas of what discipline is.

(B) Permissiveness is the most widely used disciplinary style.

(C) Most people agree on their definition of discipline.

(D) There are four disciplinary styles.

(E) Child development needs to focus on obedience to authority.

18. What is the author's purpose in writing this?

(A) To describe

(B) To narrate

(C) To entertain

(D) To inform

(E) To argue

19. From reading this passage, we can conclude that:

(A) The author is a teacher.

(B) The author has many children.

(C) The author has written a book about discipline.

(D) The author has done a lot of research on discipline.

(E) The author has at least two siblings.

20. What does the technique of reasoning involve?

(A) Persuading the child to behave in a certain way.

(B) Allowing the child to do as he/she pleases.

(C) Using force to discourage unwanted behavior.

(D) Making love conditional on good behavior.

(E) Distracting the child in order to get them to behave appropriately.

Each underlined portion of sentences 21-23 contains one or more errors in grammar, usage, mechanics, or sentence structure. Circle the choice that best corrects the error without changing the meaning of the original sentence. Choice E may repeat the underlined portion. Select the identical phrase if you find no error.

21. Walt Whitman was famous for <u>his composition, *Leaves of Grass,* serving as a nurse during the Civil War, and a devoted son.</u>

   (A) *Leaves of Grass,* his service as a nurse during the Civil War, and a devoted son.

   (B) composing *Leaves of Grass,* serving as a nurse during the Civil War, and being a devoted son.

   (C) his composition, *Leaves of Grass,* his nursing during the Civil War, and his devotion as a son.

   (D) serving as a nurse during the civil war, being a devoted son and *Leaves of Grass.*

   (E) his composition, *Leaves of Grass,* serving as a nurse during the Civil War, and a devoted son.

22. There were <u>fewer pieces</u> of evidence presented during the second trial.

   (A) fewer peaces

   (B) less peaces

   (C) less pieces

   (D) not as many peaces

   (E) fewer pieces

23. Wally **groaned, "Why** do I have to do an oral interpretation **of** **"The Raven."**

(A) groaned "Why…of 'The Raven'?"

(B) groaned "Why…of "The Raven"?

(C) groaned "Why…of "The Raven?"

(D) groaned, "Why…of "The Raven."

(E) groaned, "Why…of *The Raven?*"

Read the following paragraph and answer the questions that follow.

Microbiology is the study of tiny organisms that can only be seen through a magnifying glass or microscope. Scientists have used microbiology to help prevent and cure certain diseases. It has also been important in the development of new and better foods.

24. **What is the main idea of this passage?**

(A) Microbiology has been used to prevent and cure certain diseases.

(B) Through microbiology, scientists have made discoveries that have helped many people.

(C) Microbiology is the study of tiny organisms.

(D) It is necessary to have a magnifying glass or microscope when engaged in a microbiological study.

(E) none of the above.

Read the following paragraph and answer the questions that follow.

Many people insist on wearing "real" fur coats even though artificial furs have been available for over 30 years. It is cruel to torture animals just to be fashionable. Save an animal by wearing artificial fur coats instead of "real" ones.

25. The author's purpose is to

(A) Describe

(B) Inform

(C) Persuade

(D) Narrate

(E) Summarize

Read the following paragraph and answer the questions that follow.

Plants are very versatile living organisms. They are constantly adapting to survive in their environments. Some plants have grown spines to protect themselves from herbivores. Plants that grow in cold regions grow close to the ground to avoid harsh winds.

26. What type of organizational pattern is the author using?

(A) Cause and Effect

(B) Generalization

(C) Comparison and Contrast

(D) Simple Listing

(E) Analogy

Read the following paragraph and answer the questions that follow.

Rembrandt and Van Gogh were two Dutch painters. Both were from wealthy families. Both showed incredible talent at a young age. Van Gogh did not begin to paint seriously until he was twenty-seven. Rembrandt, on the other hand, had already completed many paintings by that age.

27. Which organizational pattern does the author use?

(A) Comparison and Contrast

(B) Simple Listing

(C) Cause and Effect

(D) Definition

(E) Description

Read the following paragraph and answer the questions that follow.

Charles Lindbergh had no intention of becoming a pilot. He was enrolled in the University of Wisconsin until a flying lesson changed the entire course of his life. He began his career as a pilot by performing daredevil stunts at fairs.

28. The author wrote this paragraph primarily to:

(A) describe

(B) inform

(C) entertain

(D) narrate

(E) analyze

29. Addressing someone absent or something inhuman as though present and able to respond describes a figure of speech known as:

(A) personification

(B) synecdoche

(C) metonymy

(D) apostrophe

(E) rhetorical strategy

Read the following paragraph and answer the questions below, selecting the best choice of the options presented.

(1) It was a cold and windy night. (2) Everyone was close around the fire in order to keep warm. (3) It was lonely for the little boy, who waited for his mother to bring him a marshmallow to toast on a stick. (4) His sister died just weeks ago and he really missed her.

30. In sentence (2), a better way to phrase "was close" could be:

(A) huddled

(B) gather

(C) stood

(D) left from

(E) none of these options are better

31. In sentence (4), the author is describing what emotion?

(A) hunger

(B) happiness

(C) coldness

(D) sadness

(E) anger

Read the following passage and answer the questions that follow.

As she mused the pitiful vision of her mother's life laid its spell on the very quick of her being—that life of commonplace sacrifices closing in final craziness. She trembled as she heard again her mother's voice saying constantly with foolish insistence: Derevaun Seraun! Derevaun Seraun!

*Derevaun Seraun means "The end of pleasure is pain!" (Gaelic)

32. The passage is written from which point of view?

(A) First person, narrator

(B) Second person, direct address

(C) Third person, omniscient

(D) First person, omniscient

(E) First person, direct address

33. To understand the origins of a word, one must study the:

(A) synonyms

(B) inflections

(C) phonetics

(D) etymology

(E) epidemiology

34. Which is the best definition for syntax?

(A) The specific order of word choices by an author to create a particular mood or feeling in the reader

(B) Writing that explains something thoroughly

(C) The background or exposition for a short story or drama

(D) Word choices that help teach a truth or moral

(E) Proper elocution

35. Which is the least true statement concerning an author's literary tone?

(A) Tone is partly revealed through the selection of details.

(B) Tone is the expression of the author's attitude toward his or her subject.

(C) Tone can be expressed in a variety of ways by an author.

(D) Tone in literature corresponds to the tone of voice a speaker uses.

(E) Tone in literature is usually satiric or angry.

36. **Regarding the study of poetry, which elements are least applicable to all types of poetry?**

 (A) Setting and audience

 (B) Theme and tone

 (C) Pattern and diction

 (D) Diction and rhyme scheme

 (E) Words and symbols

Read the following poem and answer the questions that follow.

There is no frigate like a book
To take us lands away,
Nor any coursers like a page
Of prancing poetry;
This traverse may the poorest take
Without oppress of toll;
How frugal is the chariot
That bears the human soul!

37. **How many types of transport types does the author incorporate?**

 (A) two

 (B) three

 (C) four

 (D) five

 (E) none

38. **If the words 'frigate, coursers, and chariot' were replaced with synonyms, what would the best choice of the following options include?**

(A) Train, car, carriage

(B) Train, horse, carriage

(C) Ship, car, carriage

(D) Ship, car, train

(E) Ship, horse, carriage

39. **What is a good paraphrase of "To take us lands away" that Ms. Dickinson writes in this poem?**

(A) War makes it unsafe to travel, so we can just read about places.

(B) Poems will drive us to save our souls.

(C) Books can engage us to see new things

(D) Authors can show us how to go on vacation.

(E) It shows poems are short and fun.

Read the following poem and answer the questions that follow.

Tyger! Tyger! burning bright
In the forests of the night,
What immortal hand or eye
Could frame thy fearful ymmetry? (line 4)

In what distant deeps or skies
Burnt the fire of thine eyes?
On what wings dare he aspire?
What the hand dare seize the flame? (line 8)

And what shoulder, & what art,
Could twist the sinews of they heart?
And when thy heart began to beat,
What dread hand? & what dread feet? (line 12)

40. Sinews, in the third stanza, can be best compared to:

(A) thread.

(B) a cage.

(C) rope.

(D) heart strings or emotions.

(E) burnt fire, from the second stanza.

41. Another phrase for "deeps or skies" that would fit in this poem could be:

(A) caves or planes.

(B) trees or forests.

(C) seas or air.

(D) waves or wind.

(E) oceans or lakes.

42. In line 7 of this poem, what word below most nearly means "aspire"?

(A) Soar.

(B) Plunge.

(C) Scheme.

(D) Travel.

(E) Admire.

Read the following passage and answer the questions that follow.

These are morning matters, pictures you dream as the final wave heaves you up on the sand in the bright light and drying air. You remember pressure, and a curved sleep you rested against, soft, like a scallop in its shell. But the air hardens your skin; you stand; you leave the lighted shore to explore some dim headland, and soon you're lost in the leafy interior, intent, remembering nothing.

I still think of that old tomcat, mornings, when I wake. Things are tamer now; I sleep with the window shut. The cats and our rites are gone and my life is changed, but the memory remains of something powerful playing over me. I wake expectant, hoping to see a new thing. If I'm lucky I might be jogged awake by a strange bird call. I dress in a hurry, imagining the yard flapping with auks, or flamingos. This morning it was a wood duck, down at the creek. It flew away.

43. The phrase, "like a scallop in its shell" is an example of:

(A) an irony.

(B) a simile.

(C) a metaphor.

(D) personification.

(E) euphemism.

44. The phrase "the air hardens your skin" within the context of the passage most likely refers to what?

(A) The morning air woke the character up from dreaming.

(B) The scallop shell bed the character sleeps in has opened.

(C) The air dries out the character's skin.

(D) The coldness of the room turns off the brain of the character.

(E) The air turns the character's skin cold when the cat leaves the bed.

Read the following passage and answer the questions that follow.

One of the most difficult problems plaguing American education is the assessment of teachers. No one denies that teachers ought to be answerable for what they do, but what exactly does that mean? The Oxford American Dictionary defines accountability as: the obligation to give a reckoning or explanation for one's actions.

Does a student have to learn for teaching to have taken place? Historically, teaching has not been defined in this restrictive manner; the teacher was thought to be responsible for the quantity and quality of material covered and the way in which it was presented. However, some definitions of teaching now imply that students must learn in order for teaching to have taken place.

As a teacher who tries my best to keep current on all the latest teaching strategies, I believe that those teachers who do not bother even to pick up an educational journal every once in a while should be kept under close watch. There are many teachers out there who have been teaching for decades and refuse to change their ways even if research has proven that their methods are outdated and ineffective. There is no place in the profession of teaching for these types of individuals. It is time that the American educational system clean house, for the sake of our children

45. Where does the author get her definition of "accountability?"

(A) Webster's Dictionary

(B) Encyclopedia Brittanica

(C) Oxford Dictionary

(D) World Book Encyclopedia

(E) Wikipedia

46. In the second paragraph, the second sentence can best be described as:

(A) compound.

(B) complex.

(C) run-on.

(D) a fragment.

(E) compound-complex.

47. Taite, Richard. "Five Things to Know About Recovery from Alcohol." *Psychology Today*. Web. (https://www.psychologytoday.com/blog/ending-addiction-good/201510/five-things-know-about-recovery-alcohol-or-drugs) October 16, 2015.

In the citation, 16 October 2015 provides what information?

(A) Date printed

(B) Date accessed

(C) Date placed on the Internet

(D) Date the last person accessed it

(E) None of these are correct

48. Nelson, MD., Lewis S et al. Addressing the Opioid Epidemic. *JAMA*. 13 October 2015; 314(14): 1453-1454.

The (14) refers to:

(A) the fourteenth article in the magazine.

(B) the fourteenth article published by this author.

(C) there are fourteen articles on opioids in this issue.

(D) there are fourteen authors.

(E) This is the fourteenth issue in the series, in volume 314.

49. In the *JAMA* citation previously, 1454-1454 refers to what?

(A) The number of issues this has magazine has published.

(B) How many articles have discussed opioids in the magazine's history.

(C) Page numbers for this citation.

(D) Ongoing page numbers for the table of contents in this magazine.

(E) Tagnemics

50. The word 'print' at the end of a citation is a reference for:

(A) the article is from a newspaper.

(B) the article is from a book.

(C) the article is from a periodical.

(D) the article was not accessed online.

(E) none of these selections are accurate.

51. Ciottone, Gregory et al. *Disaster Medicine,* Second Edition. Elsevier, digital. September 24, 2015. ISBN-13: 978-0323286657

The "et al" refers to:

(A) no hard cover copy is available.

(B) the content is digital only.

(C) this has been published in the United States.

(D) that Ciottone is the editor.

(E) more than one author should be listed.

52. Serra, Luigi. Domencio Zampieri, detto Il Domenichino. E. Calzone, ed. 1909. Princeton University.

Who is the editor?

(A) Serra Luigi

(B) Luigi Serra

(C) E. Calzone

(D) Domenico Zampieri

(E) Domenichino

53. Cattong, Bruce. "Grant and Lee: A Study in Contrasts." *The Bedford Reader*. 9th ed. Ed. X. J. Kennedy et al. Boston: Bedford/ St. Martin's, 2006. 258-61. Print. This is an ex-ample of what kind of citation for-mat?

(A) MLA

(B) APA

(C) Chicago

(D) Turabian

(E) None of these

54. Aloise-Young, P. A. (1993). The development of self-presentation: Self-promotion in 6- to 10- year-old children. *Social Cognition, II,* 201-222. This is an example of what kind of citation?

(A) MLA

(B) APA

(C) Chicago

(D) Turabian

(E) None of these

55. **Smith, John Maynard. "The Origin of Altruism."** *Nature* **393 (1998): 639-40. This is an example of which kind of citation?**

   (A) MLA

   (B) APA

   (C) Chicago

   (D) Turabian

   (E) None of these

Read the following passage and answer the questions that follow.

"(1) These good folk, who have only just begun to think and act for themselves, are slow as yet to grasp the changed conditions which should attach them to these theories. (2) They have only reached those ideas which conduce to economy and to physical welfare; in the future, if some one else carries on this work of mine, they will come to understand the principles that serve to uphold and preserve public order and justice. (3) As a matter of fact, it is not sufficient to be an honest man, you must appear to be honest in the eyes of others. (4) Society does not live by moral ideas alone; its existence depends upon actions in harmony with those ideas."

56. **The first sentence can best be described as:**

   (A) compound.

   (B) complex.

   (C) run-on.

   (D) a fragment.

   (E) compound-complex.

57. **The second sentence can best be described as:**

   (A) compound.

   (B) complex.

   (C) run-on.

   (D) a fragment.

   (E) compound-complex.

58. Warren, Robert Penn. *All The King's Men*. New York: Harcourt, Brace, 1946. Print. p415.

The p415 sentence can best be described as:

(A) the number of pages in the book used.

(B) the last page the reader completed.

(C) the citation for a portion referenced in the a document.

(D) the last page of dialogue in the book.

(E) none of the choices are accurate.

59. United States. Cong. Senate. Appropriations. Schedule of Serial Set Volumes. 112 Cong., 2 sess. S. Doc. 15383A. Washington DC: U.S. Senate, 2012. Web.

15383A can best be described as:

(A) amendment number.

(B) edit number.

(C) page number.

(D) volume number

(E) document number.

60. Bell, A. G. (1876). *U.S. Patent No. 174,465.* Washington, DC: U.S. Patent and Trademark Office.

This is the patent citation for:

(A) a lightbulb.

(B) train brakes.

(C) relativity.

(D) telephone.

(E) telegraph.

61. Mozart, W. A. (1970). *Die Zauberflöte* [The magic flute], K. 620 [Vocal score]. Munich, Germany: Becksche Verlagsbuchhandlung. (Original work published 1791).

The "K. 620" is the citation for:

(A) the 620th note in the musical score.

(B) opus, or work number.

(C) the number of instruments required.

(D) the number of performers required, including voices.

(E) none of these are correct.

62. Harris, Ann Sutherland (PhD). Seventeenth Century Art and Architecture. Lawrence King Publishing, 2005. pxv. The "pxv" is:

(A) the version label.

(B) the author's work number.

(C) the date in Roman numeral.

(D) the preface page number.

(E) none of these are correct.

63. "Higher education has become a central part of the process by which high-income families can seek to assure that their children are more likely to have high incomes." Taylor, Timothy. How Higher Education Perpetuates Intergenerational Inequality. March 4, 2015. http://conversableeconomist.blogspot.com/2015/03/how-higher-education-perpetuates.html Accessed August 8, 2015.

When prefaced with "61" in superscript before this phrase and listed on the same page, it would be referred to as a(an):

(A) footnote.

(B) endnote.

(C) footer.

(D) header.

(E) none of these are correct.

Read the following paragraph and answer the questions that follow.

This writer has often been asked to tutor hospitalized children with cystic fibrosis. While undergoing all the precautionary measures to see these children (i.e. scrubbing thoroughly and donning sterilized protective gear-for the child's protection), she has often wondered why their parents subject these children to the pressures of schooling and trying to catch up on what they have missed because of hospitalization, which is a normal part of cystic fibrosis patients' lives. These children undergo so many tortuous treatments a day that it seems cruel to expect them to learn as normal children do, especially with their life expectancies being as short as they are.

64. What is the author's main purpose?

(A) To inform

(B) To entertain

(C) To describe

(D) To narrate

(E) To record

65. What is the main idea of this passage?

(A) There is a lot of preparation involved in visiting a patient of cystic fibrosis.

(B) Children with cystic fibrosis are incapable of living normal lives.

(C) Certain concessions should be made for children with cystic fibrosis.

(D) Children with cystic fibrosis die young.

(E) The specific ways you must decontaminate yourself to visit children.

66. What is meant by the word "precautionary" in the second sentence?

(A) Careful

(B) Protective

(C) Medical

(D) Sterilizing

(E) Reckless

67. What is the author's tone in the previous passage?

(A) Sympathetic

(B) Cruel

(C) Disbelieving

(D) Cheerful

(E) Cautious

68. What type of organizational pattern is the author using in the selection about cystic fibrosis?

(A) Classification

(B) Explanation

(C) Comparison and Contrast

(D) Cause and Effect

(E) Entertaining

69. How is the author so familiar with the procedures used when visiting a child with cystic fibrosis?

(A) She has read about it.

(B) She works in a hospital.

(C) She is the parent of one.

(D) She often tutors them.

(E) She had it as a child.

Read the following passage and answer the questions that follow.

Disciplinary practices have been found to affect diverse areas of child development such as the acquisition of moral values, obedience to authority, and performance at school. Even though the dictionary has a specific definition of the word "discipline," it is still open to interpretation by people of different cultures.

There are four types of disciplinary styles: assertion of power, withdrawal of love, reasoning, and permissiveness. Assertion of power involves the use of force to discourage unwanted behavior. Withdrawal of love involves making the love of a parent conditional on a child's good behavior. Reasoning involves persuading the child to behave one way rather than another. Permissiveness involves allowing the child to do as he or she pleases and face the consequences of his/her actions

70. **What is the meaning of the word "diverse" in the first sentence?**

(A) Many

(B) Related to children

(C) Disciplinary

(D) Moral

(E) Racially disparate

71. **What organizational structure is used in the first sentence of them second paragraph?**

(A) Addition

(B) Explanation

(C) Definition

(D) Simple Listing

(E) Argumentative

72. What is the author's tone?

(A) Disbelieving

(B) Angry

(C) Informative

(D) Optimistic

(E) None of these are correct.

73. What is the overall organizational pattern of this passage?

(A) Generalization

(B) Cause and Effect

(C) Addition

(D) Summary

(E) Informational

Read the following passage and answer the questions that follow.

One of the most difficult problems plaguing American education is the assessment of teachers. No one denies that teachers ought to be answerable for what they do, but what exactly does that mean? The Oxford American Dictionary defines accountability as: the obligation to give a reckoning or explanation for one's actions.

Does a student have to learn for teaching to have taken place? Historically, teaching has not been defined in this restrictive manner; the teacher was thought to be responsible for the quantity and quality of material covered and the way in which it was presented. However, some definitions of teaching now imply that students must learn in order for teaching to have taken place.

As a teacher who tries my best to keep current on all the latest teaching strategies, I believe that those teachers who do not bother even to pick up an educational journal every once in a while should be kept under close watch. There are many teachers out there who have been teaching for decades and refuse to change their ways even if research has proven that their methods are outdated and ineffective. There is no place in the profession of teaching for these types of individuals. It is time that the American educational system clean house, for the sake of our children.

74. **What is the meaning of the word "reckoning" in the third sentence?**

    (A) Thought

    (B) Answer

    (C) Obligation

    (D) Explanation

    (E) Prayerful

75. **What is the organizational pattern of the second paragraph?**

    (A) Cause and Effect

    (B) Classification

    (C) Addition

    (D) Explanation

    (E) None of these things

76. **What is the author's overall organizational pattern?**

    (A) Classification

    (B) Cause and Effect

    (C) Definition

    (D) Comparison and Contrast

    (E) None of these things

77. **The author's tone in the passage on the previous page is one of:**

(A) Disbelief

(B) Excitement

(C) Support

(D) Concern

(E) Empathy

78. **What is meant by the word "plaguing" in the first sentence of the previous passage?**

(A) Causing problems

(B) Causing illness

(C) Causing anger

(D) Causing failure

(E) Causing unrest

Read the following passage and answer the questions that follow.

(1)London was our present point of rest; we determined to remain several months in this wonderful and celebrated city. (2)Clerval desired the intercourse of the men of genius and talent who flourished at this time; but this was with me a secondary object; I was principally occupied with the means of obtaining the information necessary for the completion of my promise, and quickly availed myself of the letters of introduction that I had brought with me, addressed to the most distinguished natural philosophers.

79. **The fourth word in the second sentence, "intercourse", refers to:**

(A) intimate relations between two people

(B) interactive conversation

(C) an in-depth artist's class

(D) a secondary outcome after a gift is given in Victorian times

(E) none of these options are correct

80. In the previous passage (referenced in question 79 also), what is the main theme of the selection?

(A) Travel discussions that compare where the characters have been

(B) Discussions about information gathering and solving an issue

(C) Meeting gentlemen for coffee

(D) Identifying the thought-leaders of the time

(E) How the travelers were going to spend their time in the city.

Read the following paragraph and answer the questions that follow.

"Oh, Madam Mina," he said, "how can I say what I owe to you? This paper is as sunshine. It opens the gate to me. I am dazed, I am dazzled, with so much light, and yet clouds roll in behind the light every time. But that you do not, cannot comprehend. Oh, but I am grateful to you, you so clever woman. Madame," he said this very solemnly, "if ever Abraham Van Helsing can do anything for your or yours, I trust you will let me know. It will be pleasure and delight if I may serve you as a friend, as a friend, but all I have ever learned, all I can ever do, shall be for you and those you love. There are darknesses in life, and there are lights. You are one of the lights. You are one of the lights. You will have a happy life and a good life, and your husband will be blessed in you."

81. The phase "This paper is as sunshine. It opens the gate to me." means:

(A) Madam Mina was holding a light in the next sentence that made it seem as bright as day.

(B) the character speaking has been given new glasses with which to see the sunshine.

(C) the character speaking simply has new information that is helpful to him.

(D) that he is making a joke to Madam Mina.

(E) none of these things.

82. **Using the information only presented in the selection, he tone used by the author suggests:**

(A) Madam Mina gave Van Helsing information unwillingly.

(B) one of the characters has been drinking a love potion.

(C) Madam Mina wants nothing to do with Van Helsing.

(D) that Van Helsing is making fun to Madam Mina.

(E) Van Helsing is enamored with Madam Mina because of her helpfulness.

Read the following passage and answer the questions that follow.

"Mornings, he likes to sit in his new leather chair by his new living room window, looking out across the rooftops and chimney pots, the clotheslines and telegraph lines and office towers. It's the first time Manhattan, from high above, hasn't crushed him with desire. On the contrary the view makes him feel smug. All those people down there, striving, hustling, pushing, shoving, busting to get what Willie's already got. In spades. He lights a cigarette, blows a jet of smoke against the window. Suckers."

83. **The subject in this passage is**

(A) a character, and seems to be the lead in the story.

(B) a supporting character.

(C) has the attitude of a criminal.

(D) female.

(E) has been poor his whole life.

84. **What kind of description is the author providing of this scene?**

(A) Backstory of the character.

(B) A characterization of what the character is like.

(C) A narrative, with the end of the selection giving thoughts in the first person.

(D) The unreliable narrative about a character.

(E) The author is using a persuasive argument.

85. **What types of words are "striving, hustling, pushing, shoving, bustling"?**

(A) Adjectives

(B) Adverbs

(C) Nouns

(D) Gerunds

(E) Verbs

86. **If you had to explain the phrase "crushed him" in the paragraph above and context of the paragraph, what would be the best appropriate explanation?**

(A) The city sustained him with all the opportunity available.

(B) The city called to him to be part of its life.

(C) The city complimented him for everything he has achieved.

(D) The city had energized him to get what he felt he deserved.

(E) The city smothered him with all of its offerings.

87. **The author portrays the attitude of the character toward the people on the street below as:**

(A) Condescending.

(B) Sarcastic.

(C) Affectionate.

(D) Tolerant.

(E) Encouraged.

Read the following paragraph and answer the questions that follow.

Solemnly he came forward and mounted the round gunrest. He faced about and blessed gravely thrice the tower, the surrounding country and the awaking mountains. Then, catching sight of Stephen Dedalus, he bent towards him and made rapid crosses in the air, gurgling in his throat and shaking his head. Stephen Dedalus, displeased and sleepy, leaned his arms on the top of the staircase and looked coldly at the shaking gurgling face that blessed him, equine in its length, and at the light untenured hair, grained and hued like pale oak.

88. **The likely setting for this paragraph is:**

(A) a hospital.

(B) the battlefield.

(C) Stephen's bedroom.

(D) beside the river.

(E) unable to be determined.

89. **The description of the main character's hair leads to the conclusion that he is:**

(A) a blonde.

(B) a brunette.

(C) has black hair.

(D) has grained black and white hair.

(E) is bald.

90. **The phrase "equine in its length" to describe the main character:**

(A) is complementary as horses were very valuable to soldiers.

(B) could be considered sarcastic.

(C) reveals the way Stephen feels about the main character, which is not fond or complementary.

(D) was a common description of the time period.

(E) is used repeatedly in this book.

Sample Test Essays _____

Readers will assign scores based on a matrix, or scoring guide. Here is an example outline of how both student essays will be graded on a six point scale.

SCORE OF 6: The 6 essay presents a thesis that is coherent and well-developed. The writer's ideas are detailed, intelligent, and thoroughly elaborated. The writer's use of language and structure is correct and meaningful.

SCORE OF 5: The 5 essay presents a thesis and offers persuasive support. The writer's ideas are usually new, mature, and thoroughly developed. A command of language and a variety of structures are evident.

SCORE OF 4: The 4 essay presents a thesis and frequently offers a plan of development, which is usually demonstrated. The writer offers sufficient details to achieve the purpose of the essay. There is capable use of language and varied sentence structure. Errors in sentence structure and usage don't interfere with the writer's main purpose.

SCORE OF 3: The 3 essay gives a thesis and offers a plan of development, which is usually demonstrated. The writer gives support that leans toward generalized statements or a listing. Overall, the support in a 3 essay is neither adequate nor coherent enough to be convincing. There are errors in sentence structure and usage that frequently interfere with the writer's ability to state the purpose.

SCORE OF 2: The 2 essay usually states a thesis. The writer offers support that may be incomplete. Simple and disconnected sentence structure is present. Mistakes in grammar and usage often thwart the writer's ability to state the purpose.

SCORE OF 1: The 1 essay has a thesis that is pointless or poorly articulated. Support is shallow. The language is muddled and confusing. Many mistakes in grammar and usage.

Essay 1

As a reminder, you have 30 minutes to compose your essay and type it on the computer.

Directions: Write an essay in which you discuss the extent to which you agree or disagree with the statement below. Support your discussion with specific reasons and examples from your reading, experience or observations.

Topic: Communication is the key for success.

Essay 2

As a reminder, you have 40 minutes to read these two passages and type your essay on the computer.

Directions: Write an essay in which you incorporate the two sources of information provided below. You must use both sources and you must use appropriate citation for both sources using the author's last name, the title or by any other means that adequately identifies it. Support your discussion with specific reasons and examples from your reading, experience or observations.

Assignment: Read the following sources carefully. Then write an essay in which you develop a position on whether communities have contracts to keep peace and fellow members free from harm.

Introduction: A contract is a legal agreement between people, companies, et cetera. Miriam-Webster Dictionary.

Source 1: Hobbes, Thomas. "Leviathan." England: 1651.

> Except - The final cause, end or design of men (who naturally love liberty, and dominion over others) in the introduction of that restraint upon themselves in which we see them live in Commonwealths, is the foresight of their own preservation, and of a more contented live thereby; that is to say, of getting themselves out of that miserable condition of war which is necessarily consequent, as hath been shown, to the natural passions of men when there is no visible power to keep them in awe, and tie them by fear of punishment to the performance of their covenants…"

Source 2: Golding, William. "Lord of the Flies." England: 1954.

This toy of voting was almost as pleasing as the conch. Jack started to protest but the clamor changed from the general wish for a chief to an election by acclaim of Ralph himself. None of the boys could have found good reason for this; what intelligence had been shown was traceable to Piggy while the most obvious leaders was Jack. But there was a stillness about Ralph as he sat that marked him out: there was his size, and attractive appearance; and most obscurely, yet most powerfully, there was the conch. The being that had blown that, had sat waiting for them on the platform with the delicate thing balanced on his knees, was set apart

Composition Modular Sample Test Answer Key

Question Number	Correct Answer	Your Answer	Question Number	Correct Answer	Your Answer
1	B		31	D	
2	C		32	C	
3	A		33	D	
4	E		34	A	
5	A		35	E	
6	B		36	A	
7	C		37	B	
8	B		38	E	
9	A		39	C	
10	C		40	D	
11	D		41	C	
12	D		42	A	
13	A		43	C	
14	D		44	A	
15	C		45	C	
16	C		46	E	
17	A		47	B	
18	D		48	E	
19	D		49	C	
20	A		50	E	
21	B		51	E	
22	E		52	C	
23	A		53	A	
24	B		54	B	
25	C		55	C	
26	A		56	B	
27	A		57	E	
28	B		58	C	
29	A		59	E	
30	A		60	D	

Sample Test Two

Question Number	Correct Answer	Your Answer	Question Number	Correct Answer	Your Answer
61	B		76	E	
62	D		77	D	
63	A		78	A	
64	C		79	B	
65	C		80	E	
66	B		81	C	
67	C		82	E	
68	D		83	A	
69	D		84	C	
70	A		85	E	
71	D		86	E	
72	C		87	A	
73	E		88	E	
74	D		89	A	
75	D		90	C	

College Composition Modular Rationales___

Directions: Read each item carefully, paying attention to the underlined portions. If there is an error, it will be underlined. Assume that elements of the sentence not underlined are correct. If there is an error, select the one underlined part and enter that letter on the answer sheet. If there is no error, choose E.

1. A <u>fearful</u> man, all in grey, <u>were</u> down by the river <u>standing</u> by the bunches of <u>rushes</u>. <u>No error</u>.

   (A) fearful

   (B) were

   (C) standing

   (D) rushes

   (E) No error

   The answer is B.
   Were is plural and the subject
   is singular; therefore, it should be was.

2. When our group of <u>friends</u> goes to Italy next year, we will be <u>seeing</u> many of the <u>countries</u> famous <u>landmarks</u>. <u>No error</u>.

   (A) friends

   (B) seeing

   (C) countries

   (D) landmarks

   (E) No error

   The answer is C.
   Countries is plural, but in this sentence, the word should be possessive, or country's.

3. <u>Their</u> are no walls high enough, no <u>valleys</u> deep enough, <u>to</u> keep the warriors <u>from</u> attacking the city. <u>No error</u>.

(A) Their

(B) valleys

(C) to

(D) from

(E) No error

The answer is A.

Again, the word listed - their - is possessive and here, the correct word should be the location (there).

4. <u>Whenever</u> the phone rings, the dog <u>likes</u> to run to the front door to <u>see</u> who <u>has come</u> to visit. <u>No error</u>

(A) Whenever

(B) likes

(C) see

(D) has come

(E) No error

The answer is E

as everything is right.

5. <u>Every one</u> must pass <u>through</u> Vanity Fair in order to get to the <u>celestial</u> city and receive <u>their</u> three golden eggs. <u>No error</u>

(A) Every one

(B) through

(C) celestial

(D) their

(E) No error

The answer is A.

Everyone is one word, not two (as listed).

6. Suffering <u>has been</u> stronger than all other teaching, and <u>have</u> taught me to understand what <u>your</u> heart <u>use</u> to be. <u>No error</u>

(A) has been

(B) have

(C) your

(D) use

(E) No error

The answer is B.

The incorrect verb tense is used—it lists "have" but should be "has".

7. The loneliest moment in <u>someone's</u> life is when they are watching <u>their</u> <u>hole</u> world fall apart, and all they can do is <u>stare</u> blankly. <u>No error</u>

(A) someone's

(B) their

(C) hole

(D) stare

(E) No error

The answer is C.

The appropriate spelling of "hole" in this instance is "whole".

8. I have not <u>broken</u> your heart - you have <u>broke</u> it; and in <u>breaking</u> it, you <u>have</u> broken mine. <u>No error</u>

(A) broken

(B) broke

(C) breaking

(D) have

(E) No error

The answer is B.

"Broke" is incorrect for the conjugation in the tense of this portion of the phrase; it should be broken, as it is two other times in the sentence.

Read the following paragraph and answer the questions that follow.

Mr. Smith gave instructions for the painting to be hung on the wall. And then it leaped forth before his eyes: the little cottages on the river, the white clouds floating over the valley and the green of the towering mountain ranges which were seen in the distance. The painting was so vivid that it seemed almost real. Mr. Smith was now absolutely certain that the painting had been worth money.

9. **From the last sentence, one can infer that:**

   (A) the painting was expensive.

   (B) the painting was cheap.

   (C) Mr. Smith was considering purchasing the painting.

   (D) Mr. Smith thought the painting was too expensive and decided not to purchase it.

   (E) None of these things is true.

   The answer is A.
   Choice B is incorrect because, had the painting been cheap, chances are that Mr. Smith would no have considered his purchase. Choices C and D are ruled out by the fact that the painting had already been purchased. The author makes this clear when she says, "...the painting had been worth the money."

10. **What is the main idea of this passage?**

   (A) The painting that Mr. Smith purchased is expensive.

   (B) Mr. Smith purchased a painting.

   (C) Mr. Smith was pleased with the quality of the painting he had purchased.

   (D) The painting depicted cottages and valleys.

   (E) Mr. Smith was looking to buy some paintings.

   The answer is C.
   Every sentence in the paragraph alludes to this fact.

11. The author's purpose is to:

(A) Inform

(B) Entertain

(C) Persuade

(D) Narrate

(E) Analyze

The answer is D.

The author is simply narrating or telling the story of Mr. Smith and his painting.

Read the following passage and answer the questions that follow.

One of the most difficult problems plaguing American education is the assessment of teachers. No one denies that teachers ought to be answerable for what they do, but what exactly does that mean? The Oxford American Dictionary defines accountability as: the obligation to give a reckoning or explanation for one's actions.

Does a student have to learn for teaching to have taken place? Historically, teaching has not been defined in this restrictive manner; the teacher was thought to be responsible for the quantity and quality of material covered and the way in which it was presented. However, some definitions of teaching now imply that students must learn in order for teaching to have taken place.

As a teacher who tries my best to keep current on all the latest teaching strategies, I believe that those teachers who do not bother even to pick up an educational journal every once in a while should be kept under close watch. There are many teachers out there who have been teaching for decades and refuse to change their ways even if research has proven that their methods are outdated and ineffective. There is no place in the profession of teaching for these types of individuals. It is time that the American educational system clean house, for the sake of our children.

12. What is the main idea of the passage?

(A) Teachers should not be answerable for what they do.

(B) Teachers who do not do their job should be fired.

(C) The author is a good teacher.

(D) Assessment of teachers is a serious problem in society today.

(E) Defining accountability.

The answer is D.

Most of the passage is dedicated to elaborating on why teacher assessment is such a problem.

13. From the passage, one can infer that:

(A) The author considers herself a good teacher.

(B) Poor teachers will be fired.

(C) Students have to learn for teaching to take place.

(D) The author will be fired.

(E) All of these are characteristics of fables

The answer is A.

The first sentence of the third paragraph alludes to this.

14. What is the author's purpose in writing the passage on the previous page?

(A) To entertain

(B) To narrate

(C) To describe

(D) To persuade

(E) To make demands

The answer is D.

The author does some describing, but the majority of her statements seemed geared towards convincing the reader that teachers who are lazy or who do not keep current should be fired.

15. The author states that teacher assessment is a problem for:

(A) Elementary schools

(B) Secondary schools

(C) American education

(D) Families

(E) Teachers

The answer is C.

This fact is directly stated in the first paragraph.

Read the following passage and answer the questions that follow.

Disciplinary practices have been found to affect diverse areas of child development such as the acquisition of moral values, obedience to authority, and performance at school. Even though the dictionary has a specific definition of the word "discipline," it is still open to interpretation by people of different cultures.

There are four types of disciplinary styles: assertion of power, withdrawal of love, reasoning, and permissiveness. Assertion of power involves the use of force to discourage unwanted behavior. Withdrawal of love involves making the love of a parent conditional on a child's good behavior. Reasoning involves persuading the child to behave one way rather than another. Permissiveness involves allowing the child to do as he or she pleases and face the consequences of his/her actions.

16. Name the four types of disciplinary styles.

(A) Reasoning, power assertion, morality, and permissiveness.

(B) Morality, reasoning, permissiveness, and withdrawal of love.

(C) Withdrawal of love, permissiveness, power, and reasoning.

(D) Permissiveness, morality, reasoning, and power assertion.

(E) Explore, Inform, Entertain, Persuade.

The answer is C.

This is directly stated in the second paragraph.

17. **What is the main idea of the previous passage?**

    (A) Different people have different ideas of what discipline is.

    (B) Permissiveness is the most widely used disciplinary style.

    (C) Most people agree on their definition of discipline.

    (D) There are four disciplinary styles.

    (E) Child development needs to focus on obedience to authority.

    The answer is A.

    Choice C is not true, the opposite is stated in the passage. Choice B could be true, but we have no evidence of this. Choice D is just one of the many facts listed in the passage.

18. **What is the author's purpose in writing this?**

    (A) To describe

    (B) To narrate

    (C) To entertain

    (D) To inform

    (E) To argue

    The answer is D.

    The author is providing the reader with information about disciplinary practices.

19. **From reading this passage, we can conclude that:**

    (A) The author is a teacher.

    (B) The author has many children.

    (C) The author has written a book about discipline.

    (D) The author has done a lot of research on discipline.

    (E) The author has at least two siblings.

    The answer is D.

    Given all the facts mentioned in the passage, this is the only inference one can make.

20. What does the technique of reasoning involve?

(A) Persuading the child to behave in a certain way.

(B) Allowing the child to do as he/she pleases.

(C) Using force to discourage unwanted behavior.

(D) Making love conditional on good behavior.

(E) Distracting the child in order to get them to behave appropriately.

The answer is A.

This fact is directly stated in the second paragraph.

Each underlined portion of sentences 21-23 contains one or more errors in grammar, usage, mechanics, or sentence structure. Circle the choice that best corrects the error without changing the meaning of the original sentence. Choice E may repeat the underlined portion. Select the identical phrase if you find no error.

21. Walt Whitman was famous for <u>his composition, *Leaves of Grass*, serving as a nurse during the Civil War, and a devoted son</u>.

(A) *Leaves of Grass*, his service as a nurse during the Civil War, and a devoted son.

(B) composing *Leaves of Grass*, serving as a nurse during the Civil War, and being a devoted son.

(C) his composition, *Leaves of Grass*, his nursing during the Civil War, and his devotion as a son.

(D) serving as a nurse during the civil war, being a devoted son and *Leaves of Grass*.

(E) his composition, *Leaves of Grass*, serving as a nurse during the Civil War, and a devoted son.

The answer is B.

To be parallel, the sentence needs three gerunds. The other sentences use both gerunds and nouns, which is a lack of parallelism.

22. **There were <u>fewer pieces</u> of evidence presented during the second trial.**

   (A) fewer peaces

   (B) less peaces

   (C) less pieces

   (D) not as many peaces

   (E) fewer pieces

   The answer is E.

   "Less" is impossible in the plural, and "peace" is the opposite of war, not a "piece" of evidence.

23. **Wally <u>groaned, "Why</u> do I have to do an oral interpretation <u>of "The Raven."</u>**

   (A) groaned "Why ... of 'The Raven'?"

   (B) groaned "Why ... of "The Raven"?

   (C) groaned "Why ... of "The Raven?"

   (D) groaned, "Why ... of "The Raven."

   (E) groaned, "Why... of *The Raven*?"

   The answer is A.

   The question mark in a quotation that is an interrogation should be within the quotation marks. Also, when quoting a title that is styled in quotation marks (like the title of a poem or short story) within another quotation, one should use single quotation marks ('...') for the title of this work, and they should close before the final quotation mark.

Read the following paragraph and answer the questions that follow.

Microbiology is the study of tiny organisms that can only be seen through a magnifying glass or microscope. Scientists have used microbiology to help prevent and cure certain diseases. It has also been important in the development of new and better foods.

24. What is the main idea of this passage?

(A) Microbiology has been used to prevent and cure certain diseases.

(B) Through microbiology, scientists have made discoveries that have helped many people.

(C) Microbiology is the study of tiny organisms.

(D) It is necessary to have a magnifying glass or microscope when engaged in a microbiological study.

(E) none of the above.

The answer is B.

Two of the sentences in the paragraph support that this is the main idea.

Read the following paragraph and answer the questions that follow.

Many people insist on wearing "real" fur coats even though artificial furs have been available for over 30 years. It is cruel to torture animals just to be fashionable. Save an animal by wearing artificial fur coats instead of "real" ones.

25. The author's purpose is to

(A) Desccribe

(B) Inform

(C) Persuade

(D) Narrate

(E) Summarize

The answer is C.

By mentioning that artificial furs are available and that it is cruel to torture animals, the author is attempting to convince the readers to abandon "real" furs and wear artificial ones instead.

Read the following paragraph and answer the questions that follow.

Plants are very versatile living organisms. They are constantly adapting to survive in their environments. Some plants have grown spines to protect themselves from herbivores. Plants that grow in cold regions grow close to the ground to avoid harsh winds.

26. What type of organizational pattern is the author using?

    (A) Cause and Effect

    (B) Generalization

    (C) Comparison and Contrast

    (D) Simple Listing

    (E) Analogy

    The answer is A.
    The author lists some ways in which plants have changed and the reasons why.

Read the following paragraph and answer the questions that follow.

Rembrandt and Van Gogh were two Dutch painters. Both were from wealthy families. Both showed incredible talent at a young age. Van Gogh did not begin to paint seriously until he was twenty-seven. Rembrandt, on the other hand, had already completed many paintings by that age.

27. Which organizational pattern does the author use?

    (A) Comparison and Contrast

    (B) Simple Listing

    (C) Cause and Effect

    (D) Definition

    (E) Description

    The answer is A.
    Since the author is demonstrating how Rembrandt and Van Gogh were alike and how they were different, the correct answer is (A).

Read the following paragraph and answer the questions that follow.

Charles Lindbergh had no intention of becoming a pilot. He was enrolled in the University of Wisconsin until a flying lesson changed the entire course of his life. He began his career as a pilot by performing daredevil stunts at fairs

28. The author wrote this paragraph primarily to:

(A) describe

(B) inform

(C) entertain

(D) narrate

(E) analyze

The answer is B.

Since the author is simply telling us or informing us about the life of Charles Lindbergh, the correct answer here is (B).

29. Addressing someone absent or something inhuman as though present and able to respond describes a figure of speech known as:

(A) personification

(B) synecdoche

(C) metonymy

(D) apostrophe

(E) rhetorical strategy

The answer is A.

as it is the definition of personification.

Read the following paragraph and answer the questions that follow.

(1) It was a cold and windy night. (2) Everyone was close around the fire in order to keep warm. (3) It was lonely for the little boy, who waited for his mother to bring him a marshmallow to toast on a stick. (4) His sister died just weeks ago and he really missed her.

30. In sentence (2), a better way to phrase "was close" could be:

(A) huddled

(B) gather

(C) stood

(D) left from

(E) none of these options are better

The answer is A.

Huddle means to get close, and at the end of that sentence, it describes that they were around the fire to keep warm. Thus, huddle is a better choice than B or C; D is the opposite of the activity being described.

31. In sentence (4), the author is describing what emotion?

(A) hunger

(B) happiness

(C) coldness

(D) sadness

(E) anger

The answer is D.

The end of the sentence talks about the subject really missing his sister, and there is no words that would describe anger at her being gone.
If you did not read the sentence, you may try to go off of the prior question and guess coldness, but that would be wrong. Also, happiness is the opposite of what the author is conveying and is not a correct option.

Read the following paragraph and answer the questions that follow.

As she mused the pitiful vision of her mother's life laid its spell on the very quick of her being—that life of commonplace sacrifices closing in final craziness. She trembled as she heard again her mother's voice saying constantly with foolish insistence: Derevaun Seraun! Derevaun Seraun!

*Derevaun Seraun means "The end of pleasure is pain!" (Gaelic)

32. The following passage is written from which point of view?

(A) First person, narrator

(B) Second person, direct address

(C) Third person, omniscient

(D) First person, omniscient

(E) First person, direct address

The answer is C.

All of the options can be eliminated by seeing that the author uses the pronoun "she" which is third person. There is only one third person selection.

33. To understand the origins of a word, one must study the:

(A) synonyms

(B) inflections

(C) phonetics

(D) etymology

(E) epidemiology

The answer is D.

as the definition of etymology is the study of the origins of words.

34. Which is the best definition for syntax?

(A) The specific order of word choices by an author to create a particular mood or feeling in the reader

(B) Writing that explains something thoroughly

(C) The background or exposition for a short story or drama

(D) Word choices that help teach a truth or moral

(E) Proper elocution

The answer is A.

The definition of syntax is the specific order and particular word choices of an author to convey a mood or feeling to a reader.

35. **Which is the least true statement concerning an author's literary tone?**

(A) Tone is partly revealed through the selection of details.

(B) Tone is the expression of the author's attitude toward his or her subject.

(C) Tone can be expressed in a variety of ways by an author.

(D) Tone in literature corresponds to the tone of voice a speaker uses.

(E) Tone in literature is usually satiric or angry.

The answer is E.

As all of the options A through D are relevant to the definition of an author's tone, E - a very lopsided and opinionated option - is the correct answer.

36. **Regarding the study of poetry, which elements are least applicable to all types of poetry?**

(A) Setting and audience

(B) Theme and tone

(C) Pattern and diction

(D) Diction and rhyme scheme

(E) Words and symbols

The answer is A.

Certain poems are very specific in their symbols, rhyme scheme, diction, pattern and theme. The best answer for which option is not as important to poetry is A.

Read the following poem and answer the questions that follow.

There is no frigate like a book
To take us lands away, Nor any coursers like a page
Of prancing poetry;
This traverse may the poorest take
Without oppress of toll;
How frugal is the chariot
That bears the human soul!

37. **How many types of transport types does the author incorporate?**

    (A) two

    (B) three

    (C) four

    (D) five

    (E) none

    The answer is B.

    There are three modes of transport in the poem. This is further confirmed in the next question.

38. **If the words 'frigate, coursers, and chariot' were replaced with synonyms, what would the best choice of the following options include?**

    (A) Train, car, carriage

    (B) Train, horse, carriage

    (C) Ship, car, carriage

    (D) Ship, car, train

    (E) Ship, horse, carriage

    The answer is E.

    This is an analysis question to see if you understand synonyms and is important in the composition exam. Alternative words for frigate, coursers and chariot are ship, horse and carriage.

39. What is a good paraphrase of "To take us lands away" that Ms. Dickinson writes in this poem?

(A) War makes it unsafe to travel, so we can just read about places.

(B) Poems will drive us to save our souls.

(C) Books can engage us to see new things

(D) Authors can show us how to go on vacation.

(E) It shows poems are short and fun.

The answer is C.

Books, and poems, can virtually take us anywhere that we can imagine.

Read the following poem and answer the questions that follow.

Tyger! Tyger! burning bright
In the forests of the night,
What immortal hand or eye
Could frame thy fearful ymmetry? (line 4)

In what distant deeps or skies
Burnt the fire of thine eyes?
On what wings dare he aspire?
What the hand dare seize the flame? (line 8)

And what shoulder, & what art,
Could twist the sinews of they heart?
And when thy heart began to beat,
What dread hand? & what dread feet? (line 12)

40. Sinews, in the third stanza, can be best compared to:

(A) thread.

(B) a cage.

(C) rope.

(D) heart strings or emotions.

(E) burnt fire, from the second stanza.

The answer is D.

Sinews, while it is possible that anything from A through D could be correct, the only appropriate option is heart strings. Option E is simply misleading.

41. Another phrase for "deeps or skies" that would fit in this poem could be:

(A) caves or planes.

(B) trees or forests.

(C) seas or air.

(D) waves or wind.

(E) oceans or lakes.

The answer is C.

Again, this is about comprehension of the composition and your ability to identify appropriate synonyms in context of the selection. In the other pairs, one word may be accurate but the other option is not appropriate.

42. In line 7 of this poem, what word below most nearly means "aspire"?

(A) Soar.

(B) Plunge.

(C) Scheme.

(D) Travel.

(E) Admire.

The answer is A.

This is the best choice and the other options are not appropriate synonyms.

Read the following paragraph and answer the questions that follow.

These are morning matters, pictures you dream as the final wave heaves you up on the sand in the bright light and drying air. You remember pressure, and a curved sleep you rested against, soft, like a scallop in its shell. But the air hardens your skin; you stand; you leave the lighted shore to explore some dim headland, and soon you're lost in the leafy interior, intent, remembering nothing.

I still think of that old tomcat, mornings, when I wake. Things are tamer now; I sleep with the window shut. The cats and our rites are gone and my life is changed, but the memory remains of something powerful playing over me. I wake expectant, hoping to see a new thing. If I'm lucky I might be jogged awake by a strange bird call. I dress in a hurry, imagining the yard flapping with auks, or flamingos. This morning it was a wood duck, down at the creek. It flew away.

43. The phrase, "like a scallop in its shell" is an example of:

(A) an irony.

(B) a simile.

(C) a metaphor.

(D) personification.

(E) euphemism.

The answer is C.

This is a definition type of question, and it is the only possible answer.

44. The phrase "the air hardens your skin" within the context of the passage most likely refers to what?

(A) The morning air woke the character up from dreaming.

(B) The scallop shell bed the character sleeps in has opened.

(C) The air dries out the character's skin.

(D) The coldness of the room turns off the brain of the character.

(E) The air turns the character's skin cold when the cat leaves the bed.

The answer is A.

The character describes waking up in the morning, and it is the closest rephrasing of the author's words.

Read the following passage and answer the questions that follow.

One of the most difficult problems plaguing American education is the assessment of teachers. No one denies that teachers ought to be answerable for what they do, but what exactly does that mean? The Oxford American Dictionary defines accountability as: the obligation to give a reckoning or explanation for one's actions.

Does a student have to learn for teaching to have taken place? Historically, teaching has not been defined in this restrictive manner; the teacher was thought to be responsible for the quantity and quality of material covered and the way in which it was presented. However, some definitions of teaching now imply that students must learn in order for teaching to have taken place.

As a teacher who tries my best to keep current on all the latest teaching strategies, I believe that those teachers who do not bother even to pick up an educational journal every once in a while should be kept under close watch. There are many teachers out there who have been teaching for decades and refuse to change their ways even if research has proven that their methods are outdated and ineffective. There is no place in the profession of teaching for these types of individuals. It is time that the American educational system clean house, for the sake of our children

45. Where does the author get her definition of "accountability?"

    (A) Webster's Dictionary

    (B) Encyclopedia Brittanica

    (C) Oxford Dictionary

    (D) World Book Encyclopedia

    (E) Wikipedia

The answer is C.

It is stated in the first paragraph.

46. In the second paragraph, the second sentence can best be described as:

(A) compound.

(B) complex.

(C) run-on.

(D) a fragment.

(E) compound-complex.

The answer is E.

A compound-complex sentence has two independent sentences are conjoined with the semi-colon.

47. Taite, Richard. "Five Things to Know About Recovery from Alcohol." *Psychology Today*. Web. (https://www.psychologytoday. com/blog/ending-addiction-good/201510/five-things-know-about-recovery-alcohol-or-drugs) October 16, 2015.

In the citation, 16 October 2015 provides what information?

(A) Date printed

(B) Date accessed

(C) Date placed on the Internet

(D) Date the last person accessed it

(E) None of these are correct

The answer is B.

The date it was accessed on the Internet.

48. **Nelson, MD., Lewis S et al. Addressing the Opioid Epidemic.** *JAMA.* **13 October 2015; 314(14): 1453-1454.**

The (14) refers to:

(A) the fourteenth article in the magazine.

(B) the fourteenth article published by this author.

(C) there are fourteen articles on opioids in this issue.

(D) there are fourteen authors.

(E) This is the fourteenth issue in the series, in volume 314.

The answer is E

The citation for the correct volume.

49. **In the *JAMA* citation previously, 1454-1454 refers to what?**

(A) The number of issues this has magazine has published.

(B) How many articles have discussed opioids in the magazine's history

(C) Page numbers for this citation.

(D) Ongoing page numbers for the table of contents in this magazine.

(E) Tagnemics

The answer is C.

As it lists the correct page numbers for this article in the *JAMA* periodical.

50. **The word 'print' at the end of a citation is a reference for:**

(A) the article is from a newspaper.

(B) the article is from a book.

(C) the article is from a periodical.

(D) the article was not accessed online.

(E) none of these selections are accurate.

The answer is E.

As A through D are all possibly accurate, option E is correct because you need more information to choose which print item is correct.

51. **Ciottone, Gregory et al. Disaster Medicine, Second Edition. Elsevier, digital. September 24, 2015. ISBN-13: 978-0323286657**

The "et al" refers to:

(A) no hard cover copy is available.

(B) the content is digital only.

(C) this has been published in the United States.

(D) that Ciottone is the editor.

(E) more than one author should be listed.

The answer is E.

That more than one author should be listed.

52. **Serra, Luigi. Domencio Zampieri, detto Il Domenichino. E. Calzone, ed. 1909. Princeton University.**

Who is the editor?

(A) Serra Luigi

(B) Luigi Serra

(C) E. Calzone

(D) Domenico Zampieri

(E) Domenichino

The answer is C.

As Calzone is the editor. Luigi Serra is the author, and D and E are the names and alias of the artist about whom Serra writes. Regardless of language, the citation formats are the same.

53. Cattong, Bruce. "Grant and Lee: A Study in Contrasts." *The Bedford Reader*. 9th ed. Ed. X. J. Kennedy et al. Boston: Bedford/ St. Martin's, 2006. 258-61. Print. This is an ex-ample of what kind of citation for-mat?

(A) MLA

(B) APA

(C) Chicago

(D) Turabian

(E) None of these

The answer is A.
As this is MLA citation format.

54. Aloise-Young, P. A. (1993). The development of self-presentation: Self-promotion in 6- to 10- year-old children. *Social Cognition, II,* 201-222. This is an example of what kind of citation?

(A) MLA

(B) APA

(C) Chicago

(D) Turabian

(E) None of these

The answer is B.
As this is APA citation format.

55. Smith, John Maynard. "The Origin of Altruism." *Nature* 393 (1998): 639-40. This is an example of which kind of citation?

(A) MLA

(B) APA

(C) Chicago

(D) Turabian

(E) None of these

The answer is C.

as this is Chicago citation format.

Read the following paragraph and answer the questions that follow.

"(1)These good folk, who have only just begun to think and act for themselves, are slow as yet to grasp the changed conditions which should attach them to these theories. (2)They have only reached those ideas which conduce to economy and to physical welfare; in the future, if someone else carries on this work of mine, they will come to understand the principles that serve to uphold and preserve public order and justice. (3)As a matter of fact, it is not sufficient to be an honest man, you must appear to be honest in the eyes of others. (4)Society does not live by moral ideas alone; its existence depends upon actions in harmony with those ideas."

56. The first sentence can best be described as:

(A) compound.

(B) complex.

(C) run-on.

(D) a fragment.

(E) compound-complex.

The answer is B.
The writer uses expressions such as "protective gear" and "child's protection" to emphasize this.

57. The second sentence can best be described as:

(A) compound.

(B) complex.

(C) run-on.

(D) a fragment.

(E) compound-complex.

The answer is E.
There is a semi-colon and two independent phrases with dependent clauses - this describes compound-complex.

58. **Warren, Robert Penn.** *All The King's Men.* **New York: Harcourt, Brace, 1946. Print. p415.**

The p415 sentence can best be described as:

(A) the number of pages in the book used.

(B) the last page the reader completed.

(C) the citation for a portion referenced in the document.

(D) the last page of dialogue in the book.

(E) none of the choices are accurate.

The answer is C.

The page number reference shows where the citation is located in the book.

59. **United States. Cong. Senate. Appropriations. Schedule of Serial Set Volumes. 112 Cong., 2 sess. S. Doc. 15383A. Washington DC: U.S. Senate, 2012. Web.**

15383A can best be described as:

(A) amendment number.

(B) edit number.

(C) page number.

(D) volume number

(E) document number.

The answer is E.

Congressional documents are numbered and in this citation, the abbreviation prior to the number explains this is a document number.

60. Bell, A. G. (1876). *U.S. Patent No. 174,465.* **Washington, DC: U.S. Patent and Trademark Office.**

This is the patent citation for:

(A) a lightbulb.

(B) train brakes.

(C) relativity.

(D) telephone.

(E) telegraph.

The answer is D.

As this is a patent, the name listed is the patent holder, so outside information again needs be used. Alexander Graham Bell invented the telephone.

61. Mozart, W. A. (1970). *Die Zauberflöte* **[The magic flute], K. 620 [Vocal score]. Munich, Germany: Becksche Verlagsbuchhandlung. (Original work published 1791).**

The "K. 620" is the citation for:

(A) the 620th note in the musical score.

(B) opus, or work number.

(C) the number of instruments required.

(D) the number of performers required, including voices.

(E) none of these are correct.

The answer is B.

When citing music, "K." is the abbreviation during the Classical era for the German word, Kochel-Verzeichnis, and is the "opus" (latin for "work" and followed by a number).

62. **Harris, Ann Sutherland (PhD). Seventeenth Century Art and Architecture. Lawrence King Publishing, 2005. pxv. The "pxv" is:**

(A) the version label.

(B) the author's work number.

(C) the date in Roman numeral.

(D) the preface page number.

(E) none of these are correct.

The answer is D

in reference to preface pages, which are denoted with small Roman numerals.

63. **"Higher education has become a central part of the process by which high-income families can seek to assure that their children are more likely to have high incomes." Taylor, Timothy. How Higher Education Perpetuates Intergenerational Inequality. March 4, 2015. http://conversableeconomist.blogspot. com/2015/03/how-higher-education-perpetuates.html Accessed August 8, 2015.**

When prefaced with "61" in superscript before this phrase and listed on the same page, it would be referred to as a(an):

(A) footnote.

(B) endnote.

(C) footer.

(D) header.

(E) none of these are correct.

The answer is A.

This writer has often been asked to tutor hospitalized children with cystic fibrosis. While undergoing all the precautionary measures to see these children (i.e. scrubbing thoroughly and donning sterilized protective gear—for the child's protection), she has often wondered why their parents subject these children to the pressures of schooling and trying to catch up on what they have missed because of hospitalization, which is a normal part of cystic fibrosis patients' lives. These children undergo so many tortuous treatments a day that it seems cruel to expect them to learn as normal children do, especially with their life expectancies being as short as they are.

64. What is the author's main purpose?

(A) To inform

(B) To entertain

(C) To describe

(D) To narrate

(E) To record

The answer is C.

The author states that she wonders "why parents subject these children to the pressures of schooling" and that "it seems cruel to expect them to learn as normal children do." In making these statements she appears to be expressing the belief that these children should not have to do what "normal" children do. They have enough to deal with – their illness itself.

65. What is the main idea of this passage?

(A) There is a lot of preparation involved in visiting a patient of cystic fibrosis.

(B) Children with cystic fibrosis are incapable of living normal lives.

(C) Certain concessions should be made for children with cystic fibrosis.

(D) Children with cystic fibrosis die young.

(E) The specific ways you must decontaminate yourself to visit children.

The answer is C.

The author is simply describing her experience in working with children with cystic fibrosis.

66. **What is meant by the word "precautionary" in the second sentence?**

(A) Careful

(B) Protective

(C) Medical

(D) Sterilizing

(E) Reckless

The answer is B.

67. **What is the author's tone in the previous passage?**

(A) Sympathetic

(B) Cruel

(C) Disbelieving

(D) Cheerful

(E) Cautious

The answer is C.

The author appears to simply be stating the facts.

68. **What type of organizational pattern is the author using in the selection about cystic fibrosis?**

(A) Classification

(B) Explanation

(C) Comparison and Contrast

(D) Cause and Effect

(E) Entertaining

The answer is D.

The author has taken a subject and shown how one disease affects the childrens' lives in a variety of ways.

69. How is the author so familiar with the procedures used when visiting a child with cystic fibrosis?

(A) She has read about it.

(B) She works in a hospital.

(C) She is the parent of one.

(D) She often tutors them.

(E) She had it as a child.

The answer is D.

The author states in the selection that she tutors children with cystic fibrosis.

Read the following passage and answer the questions that follow.

Disciplinary practices have been found to affect diverse areas of child development such as the acquisition of moral values, obedience to authority, and performance at school. Even though the dictionary has a specific definition of the word "discipline," it is still open to interpretation by people of different cultures.

There are four types of disciplinary styles: assertion of power, withdrawal of love, reasoning, and permissiveness. Assertion of power involves the use of force to discourage unwanted behavior. Withdrawal of love involves making the love of a parent conditional on a child's good behavior. Reasoning involves persuading the child to behave one way rather than another. Permissiveness involves allowing the child to do as he or she pleases and face the consequences of his/her actions

70. What is the meaning of the word "diverse" in the first sentence?

(A) Many

(B) Related to children

(C) Disciplinary

(D) Moral

(E) Racially disparate

The answer is A.

As it affects many areas of child development, like the ones mentioned at the end of the sentence.

71. **What organizational structure is used in the first sentence of the second paragraph?**

    (A) Addition

    (B) Explanation

    (C) Definition

    (D) Simple Listing

    (E) Argumentative

    The answer is D.

    Given the options, the correct answer is D - simple listing.

72. **What is the author's tone?**

    (A) Disbelieving

    (B) Angry

    (C) Informative

    (D) Optimistic

    (E) None of these are correct.

    The answer is C.

    The piece is informative about the topic. The other options are emotional rather than descriptive about style.

73. **What is the overall organizational pattern of this passage?**

    (A) Generalization

    (B) Cause and Effect

    (C) Addition

    (D) Summary

    (E) Informational

The answer is E.

As in the previous question, the correct answer is informational, answer E.

Read the following passage and answer the questions that follow.

One of the most difficult problems plaguing American education is the assessment of teachers. No one denies that teachers ought to be answerable for what they do, but what exactly does that mean? The Oxford American Dictionary defines accountability as: the obligation to give a reckoning or explanation for one's actions.

Does a student have to learn for teaching to have taken place? Historically, teaching has not been defined in this restrictive manner; the teacher was thought to be responsible for the quantity and quality of material covered and the way in which it was presented. However, some definitions of teaching now imply that students must learn in order for teaching to have taken place.

As a teacher who tries my best to keep current on all the latest teaching strategies, I believe that those teachers who do not bother even to pick up an educational journal every once in a while should be kept under close watch. There are many teachers out there who have been teaching for decades and refuse to change their ways even if research has proven that their methods are outdated and ineffective. There is no place in the profession of teaching for these types of individuals. It is time that the American educational system clean house, for the sake of our children

74. **What is the meaning of the word "reckoning" in the third sentence?**

(A) Thought

(B) Answer

(C) Obligation

(D) Explanation

(E) Prayerful

The answer is D.

As given in the definition—right after the word "reckoning".

75. **What is the organizational pattern of the second paragraph?**

(A) Cause and Effect

(B) Classification

(C) Addition

(D) Explanation

(E) None of these things

The answer is D.

As an explanation is the organizational pattern for that paragraph.

76. **What is the author's overall organizational pattern?**

(A) Classification

(B) Cause and Effect

(C) Definition

(D) Comparison and Contrast

(E) None of these things

The answer is E.

For the overall organizational pattern is not one of the options listed.

77. **The author's tone in the passage on the previous page is one of:**

(A) Disbelief

(B) Excitement

(C) Support

(D) Concern

(E) Empathy

The answer is D.

The author's tone is concern, or D.

78. **What is meant by the word "plaguing" in the first sentence of the previous passage?**

(A) Causing problems

(B) Causing illness

(C) Causing anger

(D) Causing failure

(E) Causing unrest

The answer is A.

Another way of saying causing problems.

Read the following paragraph and answer the questions that follow.

(1)London was our present point of rest; we determined to remain several months in this wonderful and celebrated city. (2)Clerval desired the intercourse of the men of genius and talent who flourished at this time; but this was with me a secondary object; I was principally occupied with the means of obtaining the information necessary for the completion of my promise, and quickly availed myself of the letters of introduction that I had brought with me, addressed to the most distinguished natural philosophers.

79. **The fourth word in the second sentence, "intercourse", refers to:**

(A) intimate relations between two people

(B) interactive conversation

(C) an in-depth artist's class

(D) a secondary outcome after a gift is given in Victorian times

(E) none of these options are correct

The answer is B.

An interactive conversation. While the other answers may indeed be possible definitions, context is important to select the correct answer.

80. In the previous passage (referenced in question 79 also), what is the main theme of the selection?

(A) Travel discussions that compare where the characters have been

(B) Discussions about information gathering and solving an issue

(C) Meeting gentlemen for coffee

(D) Identifying the thought-leaders of the time

(E) How the travelers were going to spend their time in the city.

The answer is E.

While B is a possible answer, the most correct and appropriate answer is E, how they are going to spend time in the city, using their time wisely.

Read the following paragraph and answer the two questions that follow.

"Oh, Madam Mina," he said, "how can I say what I owe to you? This paper is as sunshine. It opens the gate to me. I am dazed, I am dazzled, with so much light, and yet clouds roll in behind the light every time. But that you do not, cannot comprehend. Oh, but I am grateful to you, you so clever woman. Madame," he said this very solemnly, "if ever Abraham Van Helsing can do anything for your or yours, I trust you will let me know. It will be pleasure and delight if I may serve you as a friend, as a friend, but all I have ever learned, all I can ever do, shall be for you and those you love. There are darknesses in life, and there are lights. You are one of the lights. You are one of the lights. You will have a happy life and a good life, and your husband will be blessed in you."

81. The phase "This paper is as sunshine. It opens the gate to me." means

(A) Madam Mina was holding a light in the next sentence that made it seem as bright as day.

(B) the character speaking has been given new glasses with which to see the sunshine.

(C) the character speaking simply has new information that is helpful to him.

(D) that he is making a joke to Madam Mina.

(E) none of these things.

The answer is C.

As the new information was helpful to him.

82. Using the information only presented in the selection, he tone used by the author suggests:

(A) Madam Mina gave Van Helsing information unwillingly.

(B) one of the characters has been drinking a love potion.

(C) Madam Mina wants nothing to do with Van Helsing.

(D) that Van Helsing is making fun to Madam Mina.

(E) Van Helsing is enamored with Madam Mina because of her helpfulness.

The answer is E

as Van Helsing effuses complements after Madam is helpful to him.

Read the following passage and answer the questions that follow.

"Mornings, he likes to sit in his new leather chair by his new living room window, looking out across the rooftops and chimney pots, the clotheslines and telegraph lines and office towers. It's the first time Manhattan, from high above, hasn't crushed him with desire. On the contrary the view makes him feel smug. All those people down there, striving, hustling, pushing, shoving, busting to get what Willie's already got. In spades. He lights a cigarette, blows a jet of smoke against the window. Suckers."

83. **The subject in this passage is**

(A) a character, and seems to be the lead in the story.

(B) a supporting character.

(C) has the attitude of a criminal.

(D) female.

(E) has been poor his whole life.

The answer is A.

The other options are not substantiated by the items in the passage, so A is the best choice

84. **What kind of description is the author providing of this scene?**

(A) Backstory of the character.

(B) A characterization of what the character is like.

(C) A narrative, with the end of the selection giving thoughts in the first person.

(D) The unreliable narrative about a character.

(E) The author is using a persuasive argument.

The answer is C.

which is provides the definition of a narrative. Backstory describes the past and he is speaking in the present. There are no personal descriptions and there is no topic that the character is trying to persuade the reader to adopt. And lastly, the leap of assuming the character is unreliable is not supported by the passage.

85. **What types of words are "striving, hustling, pushing, shoving, bustling"?**

(A) Adjectives

(B) Adverbs

(C) Nouns

(D) Gerunds

(E) Verbs

The answer is E.

This is definition and the action words are all verbs.

86. **If you had to explain the phrase "crushed him" in the paragraph above and context of the paragraph, what would be the best appropriate explanation?**

    (A) The city sustained him with all the opportunity available.

    (B) The city called to him to be part of its life.

    (C) The city complimented him for everything he has achieved.

    (D) The city had energized him to get what he felt he deserved.

    (E) The city smothered him with all of its offerings.

    The answer is E.

    As the city was so attractive to him with options and in this selection, the character describes how the city used to be oppressive to him with its options.

87. **The author portrays the attitude of the character toward the people on the street below as:**

    (A) Condescending.

    (B) Sarcastic.

    (C) Affectionate.

    (D) Tolerant.

    (E) Encouraged.

    The answer is A.

    C, D and E are too "positive" and B is not applicable.

Read the following paragraph and answer the questions that follow.

Solemnly he came forward and mounted the round gunrest. He faced about and blessed gravely thrice the tower, the surrounding country and the awaking mountains. Then, catching sight of Stephen Dedalus, he bent towards him and made rapid crosses in the air, gurgling in his throat and shaking his head. Stephen Dedalus, displeased and sleepy, leaned his arms on the top of the staircase and looked coldly at the shaking gurgling face that blessed him, equine in its length, and at the light untenured hair, grained and hued like pale oak.

88. The likely setting for this paragraph is:

(A) a hospital.

(B) the battlefield.

(C) Stephen's bedroom.

(D) beside the river.

(E) unable to be determined.

The answer is E.
While it may seem like a battlefield, the characters on on a stairwell (and there would likely not be stairs on a field). There is no indication that they are in a bedroom or a hospital, so these answers are blatantly wrong

89. The description of the main character's hair leads to the conclusion that he is:

(A) a blonde.

(B) a brunette.

(C) has black hair.

(D) has grained black and white hair.

(E) is bald.

The answer is A.
Blonde, as the last lines describe his hair as the color of pale oak. Thus, brunette as well as black or black and white are wrong. Bald could be construed from "hued", but hue means color and other indicators also point to blonde.

90. The phrase "equine in its length" to describe the main character:

    (A) is complementary as horses were very valuable to soldiers.

    (B) could be considered sarcastic.

    (C) reveals the way Stephen feels about the main character, which is not fond or complementary.

    (D) was a common description of the time period.

    (E) is used repeatedly in this book.

The answer is C.

It is an insult. While A is true that horses were valuable, the correlation to a person's looks was not meant to be flattering. Sarcasm is not applicable in this example, and we cannot determine if it was either a common description of the time period or used elsewhere in the book.

XAMonline
The CLEP Specialist

Individual Sample Tests in ebook format with full explanations

eBooks

All 33 CLEP sample tests are available as ebook downloads from retail websites such as **Amazon.com** and **Barnesandnoble.com**

American Government	9781607875130
American Literature	9781607875079
Analyzing and Interpreting Literature	9781607875086
Biology	9781607875222
Calculus	9781607875376
Chemistry	9781607875239
College Algebra	9781607875215
College Composition	9781607875109
College Composition Modular	9781607875437
College Mathematics	9781607875246
English Literature	9781607875093
Financial Accounting	9781607875383
French	9781607875123
German	9781607875369
History of the United States I	9781607875178
History of the United States II	9781607875185
Human Growth and Development	9781607875444
Humanities	9781607875147
Information Systems	9781607875390
Introduction to Educational Psychology	9781607875451
Introductory Business Law	9781607875420
Introductory Psychology	9781607875154
Introductory Sociology	9781607875352
Natural Sciences	9781607875253
Precalculus	9781607875345
Principles of Macroeconomics	9781607875406
Principles of Microeconomics	9781607875468
Principles of Marketing	9781607875475
Principles of Management	9781607875468
Social Sciences and History	9781607875161
Spanish	9781607875116
Western Civilization I	9781607875192
Western Civilization II	9781607875208

TO ORDER   or   or

XAMonline.com

XAMonline

CLEP

Full Study Guides

CLEP College Algebra
ISBN: 9781607875598
Price: $34.95

CLEP Biology
ISBN: 9781607875314
Price: $34.95

CLEP Analyzing and
Interpreting Literature
ISBN: 9781607875260
Price: $34.95

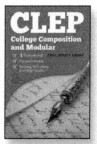

CLEP College Composition
and Modular
ISBN: 9781607875277
Price: $19.99

CLEP College Mathematics
ISBN: 9781607875321
Price: $34.95

CLEP Psychology
ISBN: 9781607875291
Price: $34.95

CLEP Spanish
ISBN: 9781607875284
Price: $34.95

n be obtained
m

024B/508/P